A CASE FOR PRAYER IN PUBLIC SCHOOLS

By Cheri Majors, M.S.

Making a case examining the enormous price we have paid for removing God and prayer from our public schools, and the consequential decay of our nation's morals and religious freedoms!

CONTENTS

Chapter	Page
1. INTRODUCTION	1
PART I. HISTORY & LEGALITIES	13
2. PUBLIC SCHOOL, CIRCA 1950's	14
3. PUBLIC SCHOOL, CIRCA 1960's	28
4. TEXTBOOKS & CIRRUCULUM	44
5. SYMBOLS & RULINGS	55
PART II. COLONIZATION & FOUNDING DOCUMENTS	65
6. CONSTITUTION & DECLARATION	66
7. SEPARATION OF CHURCH & STATE	74
8. COLONIZATION OF AMERICA	82
PART III. WORLD VIEWS & PRACTICES	85
9. HOLIDAYS	86
10. FAITHS	90
11. MORALITY	95
12. DISASTERS	101
PART IV. CONCLUSIONS & SOLUTIONS	104
13. HELP IN TROUBLED TIMES	105
14. RELIGIOUS FREEDOMS	108
15. PRAYER BACK INTO PUBLIC SCHOOLS	111

Appendix

1. REFERENCES	115
2. ILLUSTRATIONS & DOCUMENTS/REPRINTS	119

Copyright @ 2008 by Cheri Majors
All rights reserved

INTRODUCTION

Growing up in the California public school system, beginning as kindergartners at age 5 the mid-1950's, we started out each day with the Pledge of Allegiance (which included the words *"one Nation under God"*) followed by either a teacher-led or silent prayer. It did not matter what kind of prayer began our day, how it was said, or not said (as in a silent moment of prayer). It did not matter whether we were black, white, brown, freckled, or covered with a head scarf (which meant something completely different then). We were all children of God, and we instinctively knew it was correct to show reverence and respect to our Lord, the first thing every morning, at school.

The "morning prayer" either before or after the Pledge of Allegiance every day was the one defining moment, the one thing that tied us all together as brothers and sisters belonging to one large family with a much bigger purpose. We were "as one", regardless of our faith (or even the lack thereof), denomination, cultural or religious affiliations, or any prejudicial discriminations we might have brought with us from home at such an early age. Standing together in all our pronounced diversity, humbly praying (or being respectfully silent), we all felt "a part of" something much bigger, better and kinder, under God. We belonged to this great nation, blessed by God Himself, and we were just happy to be proud members of "His Team"!

Unfortunately for me, this golden-child, favored son/daughter, proud team-spirit with far-reaching purpose (unquestionably based upon solid Biblical, Ten Commandment, Golden Rule, prayer principles) would only last a short time longer. I was just ten years old in 1962, when the high court banned prayer from all our public schools. At that time in history, many of us concurrently faced yet another contradictory dilemma; which was having to learn Darwin's theory of evolution, and then be tested on it!

We would be forced to approach, learn, and embrace Darwin's theory of evolution as if it were proven to be our true beginnings, without any scientific, factual documentation, or scriptural basis, irregardless of our families' or our own beliefs or theories. Not many of my young classmates nor I, believed evolution was possible. Yet imagine our horror upon learning that Darwin himself confessed, he did not really believe in his own theory, according to the introduction in his own evolution book, On The Origin of Species, 1859.

I was personally confused about the importance placed upon learning this supposed biological life-science (certainly the "standard" scientific method wasn't employed here), of the "theory" of Darwin's evolution. The mystical theory where fish crawl out of the ocean, become land-paddling creatures, which turn magically into apes who eventually become very hairy, poor-postured yet upright-walking, monkey-men (my overly-simplified, low-priority version of one man's atheistic struggle to discover his own meaningless beginning). It sounded to me like a Jules Verne science fiction, or Edgar Allen Poe book of horror, and would certainly today make believable chapters in the Harry Potter fairytale books.

I couldn't understand why the Biblical account of "Intelligent Design" or "Creationism" was so purposefully and noticeably left out of our school academia curriculum and textbooks. And to my surprise, I've also learned that many university professors are now authoring, publishing, and ordering mass quantities of their own class textbooks, to be purchased by students taking their courses.

I have personally taken several college courses taught by professors who published their own work, and I've delighted in their Early Childhood Development/Early Childhood Education works on topics such as music, art, and developmental risk. However, many newly budding authors are purposefully and prejudicially leaving out important historical facts, such as any religious references (if the teacher has religious biases, or subscribes to another faith), and will even substitute their own beliefs or affiliations onto the pages of their own textbooks and the curriculum subject matter, sometimes changing it completely.

This unethical and self-serving behavior seems to have found a forum within our public schools and universities; instructors inaccurately teaching personal preferences as legitimate academics. When in fact, these new texts are based upon personal prejudices, opinions, or individual "theories" of those wishing to rewrite history or further their causes, without substantial proof or documentation. Is this really the "freedom of speech" our Founding Fathers had in mind? Or is this the way we want to have our children be taught in school, or the kind of textbooks we want them to be reading and tested on?

As an adult the only text, manual, or source of truth I refer to on a regular basis is the Bible, because all the other knowledgeable references I tried over the years proved flawed. I look back at my public school years with grief, as I had been cheated, academically and historically. I didn't need to learn about God, my faith, or the denomination I was baptized into from my public school teachers; as the atheist groups wrongly claimed was the case, convinced that our morning prayer was proselytizing their kids. I learned my faith at church and from my family, as did most of my classmates (although I was blessed to have a grandmother who was also a Sunday School teacher).

My classmates and I did, however need to have our nation's true historic Judeo-Christian roots and our Founding Fathers' (documented) Christian faith validated, or at least appropriately and respectfully addressed and discussed as an important part of our free nation's heritage. A heritage of religious freedom is a particularly "Christian trait", and that Christianity is the reason our country has been so blessed with abundance, and the "Creator-endowed" individual freedoms with the resultant opportunities only a free society can produce.

Sadly, these truths have been neglected at school, and now an atheistic minority believe that by removing all forms of, or symbols representing, or intelligent discussions about our documented historic Christian roots from schools, textbooks, flags, emblems, money, buildings and public gathering arenas, will somehow deny the existence of God, Christ, or truth.

The incessant demands for fairness perpetuated by the ACLU "American Civil Liberties Union" (not the opinions of, or voice of "the people" it purports to represent), and the trendy "political correctness" of the Department of Education's sanitized "anti-bias" or "tolerance" approach to public school curriculum; leave the door open to moral defiance and Christian defamation, and serves as a statement meant to appease those "threatened few" pushing their own counter-culture pervasive agendas. Yet according to the Constitution of the United States of American, our great nation was established by, and enjoys it's abundance of blessings and liberties directly from our Lord and Creator, based upon adherence to Christian principles.

Our nation's Constitution was thoughtfully and reverently outlined by our Christian forefathers, according to Biblical doctrines of God's laws for governing. Furthermore, the misquoted and misinterpreted phrase "separation of church and state", as coined by Christian Founding Father and Constitution cosigner Thomas Jefferson, is not found anywhere in the Constitution. It was not meant to be taken out of context, nor was it ever meant to take God out of any sector (public or private) of our great nation, but intended to prevent government from dictating our faith or "how" we were to worship Him. Consider the faith-based wording of, and the credited deity within our nation's founding and archived documents, such as the Declaration of Independence, and our Constitution. The actual, documented history of America was established by Christians, and claimed for God, *"from sea to shining sea"*, as embraced in the song, "America the Beautiful" (1893).

From the first landing at Cape Henry by Reverend Hunt and colonization by the Pilgrims on our Eastern seaboard in the 1600's, long before a nation, a Constitution or a Declaration, the Spanish Catholic/Christian Priests/Fathers or "Padres" were colonizing the Western coast of California in the 1700 - 1800's. Proof of this still stands, as seen by the expansive and historic California "Missions trail", memorialized from San Diego to San Francisco. The California public schools still study the missions as part of fifth grade (resident-state) history curriculum, yet the true meaning behind this exhaustive missionary urbanization project has been removed from the texts and the classrooms altogether, right along with Christmas and Easter.

Absurdly enough, the Christmas season (celebrating the birth of our Lord Jesus Christ, the only reason for the Christmas "Christ Mass" holiday), has been changed within the public school system to read "winter break" (I refuse to capitalize a holiday devoid of meaning), and is usually depicted by a cute and friendly snowman. We now tell our children that during this "winter break" we take time off school or work to do homework projects, make snowmen, and go on vacation, but lacking in purpose or any real meaning. And sadly, Easter has now become "spring break", instead of its initial purpose to worship over the fulfilled Biblical promise of Jesus' Crucifixion, burial, and resurrection.

These Christian holidays were never forced onto anyone, and few ever complained about taking time off work or school for any reason. No one was ever forced, or even asked to convert to Christianity as a prerequisite to observe these festive, joy-filled, "time-off" holidays. I personally know many families of opposing faiths who have always loved our Christian traditions of unobtrusive, yet highly celebratory worship. These same families are almost apologetic in contrast, when asked how they celebrate their year-end holidays, which include extended fasting for Ramadan, or eight days of candle burning at Hanukah, or the Hindu henna hand painting for Diwali. And by simply living in a Christian nation, they have all been privy to our delightful Christmas sounds, sights, smells, tastes, lights, gifts, and other holiday festivities, without fear of retribution, and the freedom not to celebrate with us.

The wonderful Christmas season festivities include Santa Clause (Saint Nicholas), gift exchanges, lighted houses, the smells and tastes of cinnamon and hot chocolate, singing Christmas carols, baby Jesus in a manger, poinsettia flowers and Christmas trees and stockings, flowing angels, baking homemade cookies, candy canes, church "Nativity" and "Los Posada" productions (Spanish for "the procession" of Mary and Joseph looking for a room at the inn), and in happier years past there were even delightful Christmas school plays and caroling. It is usually those who do not have any faith (atheism), who appear to be the most offended, or possibly saddened over our joyous holiday festivities, within our own Christian nation. And conversely, in other less-fortunate countries (for the citizens, not the wealthy tyrannical rulers) around the world, conversion to their national faith may be mandatory to living in peaceful coexistence within their boundaries.

Conversion to another country's faith is usually expected with threats of torture, imprisonment, beheadings, and other forms of inhumanity run rampant on the internet, and can be witnessed on world news medias such as Al Jazeera and the BBC (British Broadcasting) on a regular basis.

Whether out of fear of offending others, or facing world-wide retribution abroad or on our own soil, we have been allowing the basic Christian principles and mild-mannered, yet historical Christian symbols behind the founding, and sustaining of our great nation to be degraded and deleted. As if Christianity were a profane, four-letter word to be whispered in politically-correct compliance, or removed from our vocabulary, our nation, our documented history, our public schools, our children, and extracted from very lives. If your heart is ripped out you won't survive. However we continue to empty ourselves spiritually and morally, numbing ourselves to our loving Christian roots, and the daily affirmation of it through prayer. Sadly we are filling this void in other more tragic and destructive ways.

Increasingly, since the 1960's, United States citizens are becoming hostages of denigrating addictions to immorality and other sexual perversions, substance-abuses, and various combinations of all the above, as revealed by the epidemic proportions of drug-babies born within our country. These precious babies are usually unwanted by their unwed drug-addicted or teen-aged parents. And if they survive "full-term" (are generally born pre-mature) to "live birth", they usually end up neglected or abused and cast out into the foster care system.

That is where I get involved as a foster mom. I do my best to heal little hearts, teach them to walk, talk, read, and will try to adopt them, while bonding within my family. And although the courts will usually place these children back into the same families they were removed from in order to relieve the financial burdens of the Social Services system these little ones, usually the products of addictions, are restored back into the same toxic environments.

While trying to survive these addictive and toxic environments, youngsters are being thrown back into, there is a tendency to retain old, or develop new addictions of their own, trying to numb their pain and loneliness. The older children will usually begin by drinking, then experimenting with drugs and sex, while the younger children may develop allergies, asthma, or learning disorders, while trying to eat their way through a bad home environment, becoming obese in the process of growing up.

In 2005, the U.S. Surgeon General reported that 30% of America's children are not only overweight, but the statistics show more cases of diagnosed childhood type-two diabetes and hypertension, resulting from poor eating habits, consisting of excessive amounts of sugar and junk food addictions. In 2008, the Centers for Disease Control (C.D.C.) issued a statement, that these statistics may be declining due to health awareness campaigns and better nutritional choices being offered today by fast food restaurants. Unfortunately, the same type of campaigns are not being distributed to raise the moral consciousness of our youth, to preventing experimentation with sex, drugs, weapons, and death!

We are also becoming captives of real and imagined fears, hatreds, and the resulting fatalities brought on by the very weapons many feel compelled to carry for protection (because of our stance on "tolerance"). Just this decade Americans have been devastated by attacks on our own soil (9/11), endured sniper attacks, struggled to overcome University shootings, and are even discovering weapons in our elementary schools, to such an extent that we check (or "frisk") these kids prior to entering school buildings which we've been fencing in prison-style for years now. Because, tragically life is not valued the way it was when God's laws were revered and followed, and practiced at school.

As the wealthiest nation on earth, our lifestyles now seem to promote and perpetuate monetary and/or self-worship (self-destruction) more than the humbling Christian virtues of helping out the "poor and huddled masses yearning to breathe free", wherever they may dwell on earth. Other nations have also observed our deteriorating Christian values and practices over the years, watching us weaken and crumble from the inside out, labeling us as "infidels", or nonbelievers.

Recent world-wide events such as terrorist threats and attacks, as well as intensified natural disasters should be our "wake-up call". Yet federal, state, and local government agencies (functioning, although imperfectly) now standing on the misquoted statement about the "separation-between-church-and-state" are either ineptly unable, or blatantly refusing to help us in times of dire need. Case in point, F.E.M.A. (the Federal Emergency Management

Agency and Homeland Security), which should have been severely reprimanded or disbanded for its inexcusable failure-to-perform, after Hurricane Katrina in 2005, and was nowhere to be found after 9/11. How does the Christian view of the value of human life, in a Christian nation conflict with the very government it created? Thomas Jefferson's words that our government should not convolute anyone's religious pursuits (as the monarchy had done in England), which have been continuously taken out-of-context, have become the cornerstone of excuses used by every taxpayer-funded government agency, to stay under-involved with the people they are supposed to be working for - us!

Amazingly enough, the Bible-practicing volunteers and faith-based organizations have become our nation's newest "first-responders", helping out and taking over when disasters strike. This aid comes in the form of money, time, food, clothing, medicine, and prayers, in obedient compliance with scriptural doctrine and a true Christian love for others, as human life is valued, irregardless of faith, color, or culture. This is the American way!

If we choose to give up the strength and shield of our Christian heritage by denying God, then we also choose to give up the joys of knowing who we are, where we came from, and the predestined liberties needed to fulfill our purpose within this great and favored nation. Just like the vitamins and nutrients in our daily food, prayer is the sustaining force through which we feed our souls, and nourish our individual beliefs in God, while communing with the Creator in reverent obedience, whether silent or spoken, public or private.

My hope is that you too will come to the same conclusion I did with my own children, regarding prayer. That it inspires little minds (and big ones alike) to be accountable for their behavior, morality, and their treatment of other human beings (all of us, brothers and sisters under father God) when they know the truth about their beginnings, and reverently and obediently answer to a higher presence or calling, of our Heavenly Father God. This is only possible through prayer. Prayer not only at home and church, but in our courtrooms, the United States Senate and Congress, ball parks, hospitals, United Nations, and Universities, but beginning with our precious children in private and public schools.

PART I

HISTORY

&

LEGALITIES

"Train up a child in the way

he should go;

and when he is old he will

not depart from it."

Proverbs 22:6

Through the Country Door

Autumn 2005

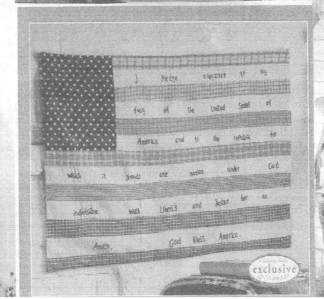

CHAPTER 2

PUBLIC SCHOOL, CIRCA 1950's

The morning bell would ring throughout the school and into every classroom, signaling the start of a new day. We knew it was time to be in our seats and ready to begin another exciting and action-packed day of learning along with our friends at public school. We were asked to stand for the Pledge of Allegiance, which we respectfully recited in unison, and followed immediately with a morning prayer, or moment of silence in which we could pray individually, or silently, depending on the teacher's preference, or school of attendance. And there were times we would pray before our patriotic pledge which, along with our upright stance and heart-felt salute, we vowed;

"I pledge allegiance to the Flag

of the United States of America,

and to the Republic for which it stands,

one Nation under God,

indivisible, with liberty

and justice for all."

According to the website "Under God Pro/Con (www.undergodprocon.org), America's patriotic oath was originally derived from the "Good Citizenship" handbook writings of a New York City kindergarten teacher, George T. Balch. As part of Blach's campaign encouraging good citizenship amongst children, and in the Americanizing of foreigners, he wrote the handbook, *Methods of Teaching Patriotism in the Public Schools*, 1887. Balch's works inspired cousins Francis and Edward Bellamy to co-author the Pledge of Allegiance for patriotic celebrations on Columbus Day in 1892, and with slight modifications, has since been faithfully recited in most United States public schools (Robertson, 2004, p.174). The Pledge of Allegiance became part of our U.S. Flag Code in 1942, and was revised in 1954, (Title 4, Chapter 1, Sec. 4 of the U.S. Code).

After World War I, World War II, the Korean War, the threat of Communism, atomic warfare, and the promptings of many nation-wide faith-based organizations and historical societies, such as the American Legion, Daughters of the American Revolution, Hearst Newspapers, and the Knights of Columbus, worried that our pledge and flag salute might be too similar to that of the atheistic Third Reich (Nazism), or godless Communistic oaths, altered them over time. A significant, yet modest revision to the Pledge of Allegiance was passed into the U.S. Flag Code, December 1954. This was after all, a post-war, God-church-family-farm, and home (modern home) era; and the Pledge of Allegiance revision was only two words, reflecting the values of the day. That "modern" revision was; from *"under God"* to *"one Nation under God"*.

The *"under God"* legislation was signed and supported by our thirty-fourth President, Dwight D. Eisenhower, who stated,

> *"In this way we are reaffirming the transcendence of religious faith in America's heritage and future; in this way we shall constantly strengthen those spiritual weapons which forever will be our country's most powerful resource in peace and war."*

President Eisenhower also voiced his faith beliefs when he said,

> *"Our government makes no sense unless it is founded on a deeply felt religious faith, and I don't care what it is."*

One year after this national, non-denominational declaration of faith *"under God"* was added to our U.S. Flag Code, African-American Rosa Parks, exercising her God-given Constitutional rights, did in fact refuse to give up her bus seat (in front) to a white man, December, 1955. We were a nation still at Civil War (a Civil Rights War), although de-segregation and integration attempts were being made nation-wide (earnestly trying to live up to our fundamental Christian-inspired, Constitutional Amendments, and newly-revised Pledge of Allegiance, proceeded or followed by prayer, at our public schools). However at that particular time, America's South was in an uproar over court mandated busing of black children and teens into predominately white public schools, to assure educational equal-opportunities for even the poorest children.

While still in elementary school in the 1950's, I remember only a few black children in our predominately white, Southern California classrooms. I was awestruck by the similarities as well as the differences between us, as this was a completely new experience for my classmates and I. Young children generally do not judge others based upon race or religion (apart from what they're taught at home), and will view each other simply as new classmates, or more importantly "a new playmate".

Attendance at public elementary school in sunny Southern California, in the 1950's, was really more like play than school, as we delighted in the variety of academia. We were not only taught the standards like history, reading, writing, and mathematics, our lessons also included science and languages, and the arts; such as modern and folk dance, classical music and instruments, drawing, painting and sculpting masters, theatre, and creative writing. We were also taught the importance of patriotism, patriotic etiquette, and how to pray a respectful, public show of faithful gratitude mixed with a personal, yet collective request for divine guidance and protection throughout the day. And that's all it was; no elaborate conspiracy bent on proselytizing the innocent with a holy-spirit-filled, tongues-of-fire church revival, that some claimed it might become.

Our morning prayer was merely a request to open our minds and hearts to receive God's infinite wisdom, divine guidance, and loving protection, as we offered our humble gratitude for his abundant provisions. It was always a simple, soft-spoken phrase or two, and/or a private moment of silence. Always tastefully presented in such a way that it could not have ever been confused with a high act of treason, nor did it ever appear to be a demonstration in the practice of passing around a collections plate for offerings/money, nor human sacrificing, nor blood-letting, nor demonic possession, nor terrorist activities. No one was ever pressured to pray, and as young children we really didn't care what your beliefs were, we liked you anyway, just as long as you respected our ways. In fact, the morning prayer was completely non-denominational and usually so neutral and watered-down, one might wonder if "those public school prayers" were of benefit to anyone at all.

In fact, just when things were getting culturally interesting, with the blending of black (African-American) children into our California classrooms and society, and could have viewed (and embraced) their gospel-charged energy-infusion, we so seriously lacked, yet needed, to breath new life into our bland morning school prayer, but didn't. Unfortunately, civil disorder ensued in the deep South. In 1957, President Eisenhower had to deploy armed federal troops to enforce a court-ordered school integration (Cummings/Wise, 2001, pg. 64).

We had entered a time in history when we had to live up to the guaranteed freedoms for all, in word and in deed. Those freedoms guaranteed not only by the United States Bill of Rights and Constitutional laws, but according to God's Biblical doctrines as handed down by Moses on the Ten Commandments, and yes, those laws (God's laws) were carved in stone (Exodus:20), (Stone, 2005, pg. 19). God's laws became the cornerstone of our governing bodies two hundred thirty-two (232) years ago, as our Founding Fathers held fast to their faith and the Ten Commandments from God, believing that they were just that - COMMANDS, not mere suggestions. *"one Nation under God"* did not mean one white nation, or a Baptist nation, or only the better-educated, as *"one Nation under God"*, but did, and in fact still does, mean all of us together, as one people, one family, *". . . one Nation under God, indivisible, with liberty and justice for all"*.

According to David Barton of WallBuilders.com, in his resource article dated and copyrighted @ 2003, *"Solving the Pledge of Allegiance Controversy"*, he quotes the Reverend Matthias Burnet, who warned us back in 1803,

> *"Ye whose high prerogative it is to . . . invest with office and authority or to withhold them and in whose power it is to save or destroy your country, consider well the important trust . . . Which God has put into your hands. To God and posterity you are accountable for them . . . Let not your children have reason to curse you for giving up those rights and prostrating those institutions which your fathers delivered to you."*

Founder and chairman of the Christian Broadcasting Network (CBN), Dr. Pat Robertson vents his anger and frustration about the U.S. Supreme Court judges' repeated misinterpretations of our Constitutional laws, and the stripping away of our nation's religious freedoms, in his book *Courting Disaster* (2005), subtitled *"How the Supreme Court is Usurping the Power of Congress and the People"*. Pat Robertson holds a juris doctor degree from Yale University Law School, and a master of divinity degree from New York Theological Seminary. He is the founder and president of Regent University, the American Center for Law and Justice, and Operation Blessing International Relief and Development organizations, and is trusted and believed by millions of Christians and non-believers alike. In his book, Dr. Robertson makes a case for our dwindling religious freedoms within the schools when he states (and I quote from p. 250);

> *"What strikes me about the abuses we've talked about in these pages is the audacity of those black-robed judges who would dare to rule that our Christian beliefs are unconstitutional when practically everything they do is unconstitutional. Declaring prayer and Bible reading unconstitutional? Saying that high school athletes and their friends and parents can't pray for safety before a football game? Who do they think they are?! By what right do these nonelected judges propose outlawing beliefs and practices that our Founding Fathers fought and died to preserve?"*

And in an article dated August 2005, from the First Amendment Center Online (firstammendmentcenter.org), by David L. Hudson Jr., entitled, *"Plaintiff in 1962 Landmark School-Prayer Case Reflects on His Role"*, Mr. Hudson cites, underneath the heading;

> *"The controversy*
>
> *In 1951 and again 1955 the Board of Regents recommended that school Boards adopt a resolution calling for a reading of the following prayer in Public school classrooms:*
>
>> *'Almighty God, we acknowledge our dependence upon Thee, and we beg Thy blessings upon us, our parents, our teachers, and our country.'"*

A simple prayer for New York public schools until . . .

Mr. Hudson continues;

> *"In July 1958, the Board of Education of Union Free School District Number 9, town of North Hempstead, adopted a resolution,*
>
>> *'that the Regents prayer be said daily in our schools.'*
>
> *School board officials said they were not violating individual rights because they included a provision in which students could opt out of the prayer with their parent's signature."*

The article states the parents sued, insisting that this simple morning prayer was a . . .

> *". . . one-size-fits-all prayer that doesn't fit the religious faiths of all people."*

How could a simple, generic prayer as quoted above not fit in with all religious faiths? In fact, the only faith this particular prayer would NOT fit with, is the godless, who do not believe in any deity. How does that qualify as a religion in our country, subject to the same religious rights and freedoms? Yet they too, are protected under our Christian-inspired Constitution with First Amendment rights.

Do we have cause to curse the generation of leaders who gave up our First Amendment religious rights, those very rights which our Founding Fathers had guaranteed for us, as warned by the Reverend Matthias Burnet over two hundred years ago? Who do we hold accountable, and how do we get our Christian (or even generic) prayers back into public schools? Were our rights to recognize God as our creator and benefactor, within our own Christian-founded nation, and in our own public schools traded away, or seduced by a mythological land the media so fondly remembers and refers to as "Camelot"?

So enamored by our nation's youngest "First Family", and first Catholic (a Christian faith) President in the history of our nation, from one of the most powerful and politically influential families of the time, President John F. Kennedy (J.F.K.) was voted into office, in the 1960's. We barely even noticed God was being marched right out of our schools, and Christian values and historic data were being trampled on, within our own nation. In an attempt to counter the nation's (unfounded) fears of Catholicism (Alee, 1986, p. 979), the courts swung to the other extreme.

In an article on the "American Atheist" website (atheists.org), by David Lee, titled "A Decline in American Culture Due to Lack of Religion?", only cites the infamous 1960's court cases (which I chronicle over the next several pages), removing prayer and Bible reading from public schools. Mr. Lee tries to either make a case for, or is in defense of these unprecedented removals, recklessly suggests;

> *"Critics of these decisions often cite the early 1960's as a benchmark in American culture which*
>
> *'kicked God out of our schools',*
>
> *resulting in a corresponding decline in morality. Everything from rising rates of teen pregnancies, drug abuse, juvenile violence and other behaviors have been cited (often with little supporting evidence) as the result."*

Unfortunately the 1940's and 1950's Supreme Court case rulings began the erosion of our religious freedoms, leading to the sequential 1960's morals decline in our nation, as we ultimately took prayer out of our public schools, and God along with them. With the expansive data on crime, morality, and divorce statistics going back to the 1920's and prior, the data in this article lacks the corresponding chronological court case rulings, and the deficiencies are noteworthy. Yet Mr. Lee's article concludes;

> *"From the statistical evidence, there is little to support the claim that that the Supreme Court rulings in the early 1960's which addressed the problem of unison prayer and Bible-verse recitation in public schools was a significant and direct contributor to crime rates, serious violence, or divorce . . .*
>
> *There seems nothing to suggest that these problems were triggered by removing prayer and Bible-verse recitation from the nation's public schools."*

David Lee sums up his article offering no ideas nor solutions for solving the "American cultural" problems (and maybe that's the atheist way), yet he continues his conclusion;

> *"Many people look back to 1961 and yearn for the 'good old days' prior to the Vietnam War, before the Kennedy killing and exploding rates of illicit drug use, divorce, and broken families. Putting the Ten Commandments, prayer, or the Bible into public schools, though, will not be the magic solution to these problems . . . They did not help then, and it is unlikely that they would help now."*

Based solely upon the statistical data within this article, the facts (case by case) disagree. Those applicable court cases and decisions from 1790 to 1963, are listed on the following pages, so you can see the facts for yourself and come to your own conclusions.

A BOOK OF FAMOUS POEMS

For Older Boys
and Girls

◆

Compiled by Marjorie Barrows
Editor, "Child Life"

Illustrations by Janet Laura Scott

◆

Copyright 1931
WHITMAN PUBLISHING CO.
RACINE, WISCONSIN
Printed in U. S. A.

Beatitudes

Blessed are the poor in spirit: for theirs is the Kingdom of heaven.

Blessed are they that mourn: for they shall be comforted.

Blessed are the meek: for they shall inherit the earth.

Blessed are they which do hunger and thirst after righteousness: for they shall be filled.

Blessed are the merciful: for they shall obtain mercy.

Blessed are the pure in heart: for they shall see God.

Blessed are the peacemakers: for they shall be called the children of God.

Blessed are they which are persecuted for righteousness' sake: for theirs is the kingdom of heaven.

Blessed are ye, when men shall revile you, and persecute you, and shall say all manner of evil against you falsely, for my sake.

Psalm 91

He that dwelleth in the secret place of the most High shall abide under the shadow of the Almighty.

I will say of the Lord, He is my refuge and my fortress: my God; in him will I trust.

Surely he shall deliver thee from the snare of the fowler, and from the noisome pestilence.

He shall cover thee with his feathers, and under his wings shalt thou trust: his truth shall be thy shield and buckler.

Thou shalt not be afraid for the terror by night; nor for the arrow that flieth by day;

Nor for the pestilence that walketh in darkness; nor for the destruction that wasteth at noonday.

A thousand shall fall at thy side, and ten thousand at thy right hand; but it shall not come nigh thee.

RELIGION/PUBLIC SCHOOL COURT CASES BY DATE

1790, to 1940

Only 12-15 cases which could have been classified as freedom-of-religion cases, most of which were handled individually by the state, as the Constitution framers gave the "High Court" a very small role in this area, unless the Federal Government was directly involved (Faith & Action, "Cantwell Case", 2005, New).

1931, United States v. Macintosh

Supreme Court declared *"We are a Christian people . . . According to one another the equal right of religious freedom, and acknowledging with reverence the duty of obedience to God."* (Robertson, 2004, p. 170).

1940, Cantwell v. Connecticut

Jehovah's Witnesses as an organized religious group refused to comply with state and local ordinances requiring permits prior to soliciting money door-to-door, and was taken to the Supreme Court. Set the precedent or standard by which the Supreme Court now rules over religious cases (took power away from states, transferring it to the Supreme Court, and basically "federalized" religious law, with loss of religious freedoms). This case was cited with regard to both 1962 and 1963 prayer and Bible reading in public schools, where the Supreme Court gave itself the ultimate power to decide (Faith & Action, "Cantwell Case", 2005, New).

1947, Everson v. Board of Education

> Justice Hugo Black establishes the infamous "wall of separation between church and state" (in his own interpretation of the establishment clause of the First Amendment); saying neither the state nor Federal Government can set up a church or show favor to any one faith over another, while the court upheld a local ordinance authorizing funds for transportation costs of New Jersey students to attend their Catholic school.

1948, McCollum v. Board of Education

> Court rules, religious instruction on school property, in violation of the establishment clause and strikes down programs with teachers coming onto school grounds to teach religion to willing participants.

1952, Zorach v. Clauson

> Court upholds programs for students to be released from classes to go to religious instruction class "outside" of school classrooms (better known as "release-time" case).

1954, Brown v. Board of Education

> Court orders desegregation of public schools, bussing blacks into predominately white schools, to end segregation.

<u>1962, Engle v. Vitale</u>

>Banned Board of Regents non-denominational prayer from public schools; Supreme Court cited Cantwell case as precedent (Faith & Action, "Cantwell Case", 2005, New).

<u>1963, Murray v. Curlett</u>

>Supreme Court bans school prayer and Bible verse reading in the classrooms, citing 1940 Cantwell case as precedent (Faith & Action, "Cantwell Case", 2005, New).

<u>1963, Abington School District v. Schempp</u>

>Court bans Bible reading from public schools except for history and comparative religious studies, citing 1940 Cantwell case as precedent (Faith & Action, "Cantwell Case", 2005, New).

These court-case listings set a "precedent" on their own, showing that the religious issues taken away from the states and put into the hands of the Supreme Court, (in the removal of God, prayer, and Bible scripture from our public schools) not only signaled a devastating decline in our nation's morality, along with rising crime rates among juveniles, and overall crime statistics, but marked the end of our Christian roots within the public school systems. This was the beginning of the demoralizing "Psychedelic '60's".

Walt Disney's Pinocchio

Pleasure Island was full of rides and sweets. The boys did whatever they wanted to do. Pinocchio made friends with a bad boy named Lampwick.

CHAPTER 3

PUBLIC SCHOOL, CIRCA 1960's

The 1960's were certainly some of the most interesting times of the last century, colorful in every aspect. Sadly, it was also the decade we officially removed God and His word (the Bible) out of our classrooms, our assemblies, our textbooks, our schools, out of our United States history, as well as out of our hearts and lives, with disastrous results. This was the era of the "Psychedelic 60's", one which we are still struggling to recover from, an era of which I have first-hand knowledge. I was a part of the generation that "dropped-out" of almost everything worthwhile, and "turned-on" to horrible self-inflicted atrocities, all while searching to re-find God and help make a better world, as we didn't trust how the adults were running and ruining our blessed nation.

My generation was given "carte-blanche" permission to rebel against, and openly defy every moral value and holy virtue by which our parents were privileged enough to have been raised with, yet didn't seem to appreciate, nor support. While our parents and our nation stood by idly and silently, the Supreme Court repeatedly ruled hostilely against every single faith-based issue for us, their children (the very faith responsible for our country's inception and existence). Was this really in our country's best interest? Who was making these less-than-coherent decisions for us anyway? We, the "baby boomers" (millions of us), were then coming "into our own", and we all had "E-tickets" (Disneyland's wildest, most expensive, and incredible rides) to paradise, or so we thought.

In Disney's classic cartoon tale of Pinocchio (the puppet-boy), he tried everything he could to become the "real" boy his father, the puppet maker wanted. Pinocchio was told to stay in school and not be lured away to Pleasure Island, where all the young boys were tempted to go. Once there, seduced by all the fun and lack of any parental controls, their behavior became so "donkey-like" that they actually became donkeys. As these "bad-boys" didn't want to go to school, so they spent their days eating sweets, riding on the carnival rides, and smoking cigars while playing pool in the pool halls on Pleasure Island.

Their unspeakable donkey transformations are almost unnoticeable at first; just a slight laughter bray of *"hee-haw"*, while the ears grew pointier and longer (Disney, 2000, p. 23). However it's not until they notice tails beginning to grow on their backsides, with noses jutting out to become donkey faces, that Pinocchio knew he and his "bad-boy" friend had actually become donkeys. They both realized it was too late to turn back, the damage had already been done.

As a young child, I can remember my own terror while viewing this timeless classic, at the horrific proposition of this actually happening to Pinocchio or worse, to be in his shoes and being cognizant of morphing into a donkey! And Pinocchio was just the child's version of the classic horror flick "The Island of Dr. Moreau", boasting black bull-nosed men and other unspeakable cross-bred monster-creatures.

It would appear that our courts, parents, public school officials, and politicians were really trying to re-create these same monstrous scenarios, with us, their guinea pigs, or "donkeys", but we were their children! Without the familiar morning prayers in class, with the rest of our classmates, answering to someone higher (God), to whom we were accountable to for our thoughts and actions, we were instead given governmental and court-sanctioned permission to be wild donkey-creatures, and do whatever we wanted to do, so we did! What kid or teenager wouldn't? I don't really believe that my generation was rebelling against societal norms, but more, rebelling because we had no controls, no boundaries. They were stripped away, right along with God.

Children need boundaries to feel safe and loved, and it is natural for them to test those boundaries, to discover when and where the line is going to be drawn. As the judicial lines were becoming fainter, along with the 1960's space program, T.V. in the classroom, the first topless bathing suit, the Beatles, and our beloved First "Camelot" Family (President J.F.K., Jackie, Jon Jon, and Carolyn Kennedy), set the tone for the new decade. It was going to be a wild ride, yet we hadn't thought about the repercussions, even noticed the slight *"hee-haw"* donkey bray hidden within our drug-induced stupor, nor our pierced and pointed donkey ears emerging, while we innocently chanted unknown mantras of Buddhist, Hindu, and Hare-Krishna origins. The Psychedelic Experience, "A novel based upon a Tibetan Book of the Dead" by Timothy Leary, father of the "LSD acid-trip-experience", was touted the Bible of the '60's counter-culture movement. As the religion-in-school court cases of the 1940's and 1950's had already laid the ground-work for the complete removal of God (through prayer and Bible readings) from our public schools in the early 1960's.

In the 1962, and 1963, Supreme Court cases; Engle v. Vitale (banning non-denominational prayer from public schools), Murray v. Curlett (banning school prayer and Bible verse reading in classrooms), and Abington School district v. Schempp (banning Bible reading from public schools except for history/comparative religious studies), we had publicly denounced God and His word, as we removed all traces of Him from our schools. In the process, robbing us and the following generations of public-school-attending children.

We were now noticing tails growing on our backsides, our noses forming into donkey faces, and unfortunately, there was no turning back. Then just days before Thanksgiving holiday, November 1963, our beloved President John F. Kennedy was shot and killed. This tragedy was followed by the 1968 assassinations of both his brother, Presidential Candidate, Robert Kennedy, and the Civil Rights Leader, Reverend Dr. Martin Luther King, who could now only dream of black and whites living together peacefully. Sandwiched in between these monumental assassinations (1965) was the Vietnam War, which no one wanted anything to do with at that time. The natives (we, the donkey-kids), were getting restless and things were turning ugly.

"Draft dodgers" fled the country or joined religious cults to avoid any form of participation in the Vietnam War (a war we couldn't win), while others drank and did mind-altering drugs, and all the while crime rates were rising and juvenile crimes were spiraling out of control. The gruesome Manson killings happened right here in Southern California in the late 1960's (and the authorities are still digging for bodies on his desert ranch, while repeatedly denying his petitions for parole from jail). Divorce rates soared in the 1960's, and teen pregnancies were beyond what we'd seen previously, due to the "free love" sexual practices of the day. While all this was going on around us, school biology/science classes were introducing us to the "modern" scientific "theory" of Darwin's evolution of the species, and we were required to learn and be tested on it's illogical and unsubstantiated content, or fail the course.

One state, acting independently chose not to teach evolution, and in the 1968, Epperson v. Arkansas case, the Supreme Court struck down the state of Arkansas' decision not to teach the evolution of humans in public schools. So here we are in the 1960's, a nation at war with Vietnam, God, and each other. So what possible importance could a non-Biblical "theory" of evolution hold for any of us? As a matter of fact, this "theory" turns out to be the major focal point or springboard used for every single biological science course in this country, right up to this day. And it is nothing more than a fantasy accounting!

Darwin's theory of evolution is embraced in mainstream scientific academia as fact or truth, when in fact, it has always been a flawed theory, one in which the self-professed "naturalist", Darwin himself, claimed not to believe. He asked his readers and critics to have an open mind and stretch across the gaps (my own paraphrasing) of his "Introduction" to; On the Origin of Species, all the way back in the mid-1800's. How did we get so far off course that our most brilliant scientific minds were acknowledging and agreeing with this outlandish "theory"? Yet one (possibly more), who was outspoken at that time, in his belief about God as the Creator of the Universe, was Albert Einstein.

One of the greatest scientific minds of our century, Nobel Peace Prize Winner and Nuclear Physicist, Albert Einstein, born in Germany to a secular Jewish family, yet attended a Catholic elementary school where he took a religious-ed class probably equivalent to a Catechism class, and loved it! Then attending an "enlightened" high school near Munich (prior to the Nazi explosion) emphasizing mathematics, science, linguistics, and religious-ed teachers to provide special instruction for the Jewish students, where young Albert quickly developed a passionate zeal for Judaism and it's strictures in detail, composing and singing his own hymns for glorifying God (Isaacson, 2007, p. 16). Einstein was guided by his faith, worn lightly and with a twinkle in his eye, in a God who he claimed wouldn't play dice by letting things happen by chance (Isaacson, 2007, p. 4). He retained from his religious youth a profound reverence for the harmony and beauty of the mind of God as it was expressed in the creation of the universe and it's laws (Isaacson, 2007, p. 20).

Einstein's theories of relativity for energy, gravity, mass, time, and space were widely accepted into the scientific arena in the 1920's, and beyond, and were in our school science books in the 1960's. His theories were proven, as he tried to explain mathematically the physics of God's Universe. On the other hand, Darwin's writings, On the Origin of Species (1859), a "theory" which was never compiled in an effort to explain God's creations according to His word, but rather an awkward attempt to deify or prove "Anglo-supremacy" over other, "darker" races, as spouted in his last and final work, Decent of Man (1871), according to the disturbing, chapter seven titled, "On the Races of Man" (read for yourself at www.Infidels.org/Library/Historical). Hitler, disturbed leader of Nazi Germany, was also a big Darwin fan, seeing the Jewish people in this same inferior light. Darwin's works are not only racially motivated, but in direct violation of God's words and laws, and the writings of the Founding Fathers of the United States Constitution, and our Bill of Rights.

Both Christian Biblical and American Constitution teachings are: to treat others equally and to regard one another as neighbors or family. Which takes us back to the whole idea of the Pledge of Allegiance, and the controversial line, *"one Nation under God"*. Yet our public schools, teachers, and school district officials have been shoving "evolution" and academia down our throats, attempting to brainwash us away from our heritage of God's benevolent "Intelligent Design" or Divine "Creationism", which gives each one of us a significant purpose for being here; part of God's larger (and much more exciting) plan for our lives.

Without a purposeful reason for being here, as Darwin's evolutionary/survival-of-the-fittest doctrine would have us believe, mere accidents or mutations of a lower primate life-form, there is simply no accountability for one's actions. How convenient is that? By the end of the '60's without our non-denominational prayer, God, or Bible reading, children were being forced to study evolution as scientific fact, and were tested on it, under threat of failing the course or having to repeat a grade. It was not even a debatable topic back then.

This was not only unreasonable treatment, it was an insult to the very heritage upon which our freedom in this great nation was founded. Possibly we (the children effected) had had enough, and as a new '60's generation we were searching to reclaim our severed ties to God and His word. We were tired of the hypocrisy and lack of concern from our elders, i.e.; self-proclaimed "liberated" (adulterous "swinger") parents, corrupt politicians and businessmen, complacent school officials, lack-luster teachers, boring and/or abusive clergy, etc. Didn't anyone care how we were going to turn out?

The 1960's ushered in a generation of hippies, searching for God through drug highs, and reaching out to others with "free love" (which wasn't free at all). Hippies traditionally did not do well in school, nor did they continue going to school, yet they seemed to embrace each other, black, white, handicapped, ugly, smart, or stupid, with a love and concern they were not getting from traditional authority figures, as witnessed at the many "love-ins", "sit-ins", "peace" rallies/demonstrations, and camp-site rock concerts. And I believe our rebellion was to make a "better way", and started innocently, with good intentions towards a touted peace, love, and honesty; a very dark side began to emerge, like a cancer growing amongst our society-at-large.

This dark side was manifested through drug and alcohol abuse, cult formation and participation, unwanted pregnancies, divorces, crime, and an overall degeneration of society. Possibly making a case for reverse-evolution, or "de-evolution", the seemingly degenerate inspiration for a strange 1980's, rock/pop group called "Devo". This "de-evolved" music group performed with jerky, robot-type movements, while balancing upside-down orange flower pots on their heads, and we loved them! But where was Darwin when we could have really use his "naturalist" explanation for this societal "de-evolving"?

My own simplistic explanation for our rapidly degenerating society in America was the removal of God and all His glory. And though generations prior to 1960, had their share of unplanned or unwanted pregnancies, many were already married, or got married, or the babies were placed for adoption, but not the case with Margaret Sanger's, "Planned Parenthood" and it's growing popularity. Although her original intent was basically the extermination of the "inferior" classes/races (in particular "blacks", as Ms. Sanger believed they were reproducing too quickly), we too were shamelessly able to take advantage of all the free services provided at Planned Parenthood, and "Free Clinic" in the 60's, like birth control and (almost legalized) abortion, to correct the "mistakes of our new-found "free-love" lifestyles.

Free-love in the 1960's was due in large part to the prevalent alcohol, and abusive drug use. Alcohol consumption, which was the party-maker of past generations was no longer the mind-altering substance of choice, it was now hard-core psychedelic drugs like L.S.D., mescaline, heroine, and peyote. Smoking pot (marijuana) was as common as smoking cigarettes in the 60's.

Mix together teen pregnancies with drugs and you produce several generations of drug-addicted babies. Mix drugs, alcohol, parties, cults, divorce, and free-love, you will get infanticide, death, disease, and destruction. Statistics show crime rates escalating in the late 1950's, on into the 1960's, and it continues rising today. Conversely, school academic test (S.A.T.) scores have been consistently declining since the 1960's (when God, prayer, and the Bible were removed from public schools), until today 2008, the United States only ranks 65th in literacy, world-wide, shamefully above only, many 3rd world nations.

Some of the current religious/school, and other court cases pending, and before the Supreme Court today simply prove how essential it is to get prayer, the Bible, and our Christian heritage back into out public schools. In January 2006, the high court ruled against the state of Pennsylvania's "Intelligent Design" case, and as it was reported on the FOX station's nightly news, news anchor John Beard reported that the presiding judge had unintelligently stated;

> *". . . intelligent design is not science, but religion, which makes it unconstitutional!"*

Since when did religion become unconstitutional? Did they pass a new law and I missed it? Did anyone check the presiding judge's credentials? And how did he actually graduate from law school, without learning the Constitution? I sure had to learn the Constitution in my government classes, and it doesn't say anywhere that religion is unconstitutional. Or worse . . . am I breaking this judges' personal Constitution or private laws he might keep on his books, because I raise my family with religion? Where is "Big Brother", and is he still watching? Possibly this particular judge went to public school in the 1960's (after the removal of God and prayer), and therefore doesn't know about the numerous religious references to God found in our U.S. Constitution.

Or perhaps this judge doesn't believe in God, or worse yet, is a self-proclaimed "Naturalist" like Darwin, or Margaret Sanger. Whatever the problem with his judicial fortitude (or lack thereof), he ruled against God himself, and might want to take a few night classes to inform him/herself of the many facets to our Constitutional Preamble, and our Christian historical roots. Aren't foreigners required to take a class to learn the Constitution prior to citizenship? Or maybe he/she simply ruled in favor of the vocal minority and did not want to muddy the political or ACLU waters, for the sake of those few non-believers in our country. Keep in mind this is the same ruling body who shot down child pornography laws, without respect for our children, or their safety. And I don't really want to get into the infanticidal abortion issues, or same-sex marriage amendments, as I currently live in the second state allowing the later, which was blasted all over the local and national news for our children to see (they couldn't miss it, whatever station they flipped the TV on to).

How did the perversion get so far out of control, that there are no laws protecting our children from moral/social deviates, under the guise of "freedom of speech"? Could we trace any of this back to removing God and the Bible, the only real source of true moral values, from our school rooms and all the way up to our court rooms?

Now let's examine the crime rate statistics up to, and through the 1960's. The Supreme Court rulings (with explanations) are found at the end of chapter two, and as you can probably guess by now the crime rates and divorce statistics closely parallel these "religion-out-of-school" cases. We'll start with the 1931 case (United States v. Macintosh), one of the last times the Supreme Court ruled in favor of God, boasting,

"We are a Christian people..."

Simple enough, yet over the years we became too trusting, and far too complacent about our God-given rights. According to the long "American Atheist" article I quoted in chapter 2, which was researched and prepared by David Lee (his statistics from the World Almanac), divorce rates had been increasing from the early 1900's, at an average rate of 12.62% (per 100 marriages) per year from 1900, to 1940. In 1940, (Cantwell v. Connecticut), the case which the supreme Court has cited as "precedent" for all three rulings from the 1960's (removing God from public schools), sent divorce rates soaring to 30% (per 100) in 1945, and that's almost an 82% increase from 1940!

The divorce rate averaged approximately 26% (per 100) yearly, between 1940, and 1965. And that is more than double the average divorce rate, prior to 1940, and it continues to grow. In 1970 the divorce rate again hit almost 33% (per 100 marriages), and on up to 50% (per 100) in 1976, up four times as much from the 1900-to-1940's, divorce rate averages which were a low 12.62%! Crime rates also began surging with every Supreme Court case siding against God, religion, and the Bible, especially in our schools.

The "American Atheist" article goes on to site the Colliers Yearbook on crime statistics for 1959, noting that crime was at an all-time high, 69% higher than 1949, and 128% higher than 1940. Please refer to the court cases at the end of chapter two, for brief explanations on the case-by-case rulings, however, I will cite the cases and years so you can see for yourself the accelerating, yet seemingly coincidental and inconsequential (atheistic and academic views) crime rates. I reiterate, these are all cases which take God, prayer, the Bible, and any form of religious instruction out of our schools.

Those cases are; 1940 - Cantwell v. Connecticut, 1947 - Everson v. Board of Education, 1948 - McCollum v. Board of Education, 1952 - Zorach v. Clauson, 1954 - Brown v. Board of Education, which was the court-ordered desegregation of public schools, and the ensuing rioting, and violent crimes. Which eventually lead up to the "Watts Riots" in Los Angeles, California, in the 1960's, nationwide "peace" marches on Washington D.C., led by Reverend Martin Luther King, and more rioting after his assassination. Coincidently, the background of Justice Hugo Black, who presided over the 1947 - Everson v. Board of Education case, may offer some insight for the escalating racial tensions of the day.

Justice Hugo Black, better known for his misconception, yet judicial enforcement of, Thomas Jefferson's infamous line from his letter to the Baptists, *"wall of separation"*, which has been repeatedly debated on TV news programs, a CBN TV news segment about Supreme Court nominees (January, 2006), and I quote Pat Robertson;

"Justice Black's only credentials prior to sitting on the Supreme Court of the United States was the Klu Klux Klan!"

How could this be? What kind of country did we live in when I was just a child? The kind of country and world which most of us, growing up in the 1960's, wanted to try and change for the better. I think most of us just went about it the wrong way, and are now trying even harder to make a real difference for humanity.

Unfortunately, the 1940 - Cantwell v. Connecticut, precedent-setting case by which the Supreme Court rules over religious cases, taking power away from individual states, was used to help decide against God, prayer, and Bible reading in public schools. Those last three pivotal 1960's cases were; 1962 - Engle v. Vitale, 1963 - Murray v. Curlett, and 1963 - Abington School District v. Schempp, and our nation went into a moral meltdown, and crime siege.

As a Child Development and Early Childhood Education Major, I can remember a small paragraph in one of my many undergraduate textbooks, on early education (preschool), which I have not been able to get out of my head. That simple, yet powerful paragraph spoke about the major complaints of parents and teachers, regarding their children in public school in the 1940's, and 1950's, which were gum-chewing, and talking out-of-turn in class. Then comparing them to the complaints of parent and teachers, about public school children in the late 1960's, until now (after removing God), and those complaints were (and still are today) more like a police rap-sheet; they include death, weapons, gangs, violence, perversion, drug and alcohol abuse, teen pregnancies, etc.

Parents blame the teachers and administrators for lack of school discipline (or sue for excessive discipline), and teachers/administrators blame the parents for lack of home discipline, all the while the police and F.B.I. are making arrests on our campuses. By the late 1990's, gun violence was responsible for 35,000 deaths a year, with one inner-city school district reporting one-fifth of their junior high school students carried a weapon, and almost half the students had had a friend or family member shot, and news headlines report killings by children ages 11 - 15, shooting classmates, teachers, and parents (Hanna, 1999, pg.5).

Pastor Greg Laurie of Harvest Christian Fellowship Church, in Riverside, California, (one of the nation's largest churches), wrote an article titled "Spiritual Education" (Inland Empire

Family Magazine, December, 2004) discussing parenting, he says;

> *"Parenting is not simply passing down a set of 'rules' to live by. It is not some 'casual' responsibility that places the burden of teaching morals or virtue on the schools or the church. It is a God-given responsibility . . . and a gift."*

It is up the to parents to indoctrinate their children into the family faith, and to teach them morals and virtues, which the public schools need to reinforce daily through prayers with the children. Greg Laurie continues;

> *"Teaching 'religion' is not enough. Our children need to see that our faith is personal and active, not something we reserve for one day of the week. We honor and look for the hand of God in every aspect of our lives."*

So too, must we look forward and beyond our continued rebellion of the 1960's, and try to do those things which will honor God in every aspect of our lives, whether home, school, work, courtroom, or voting precinct. We can learn from our mistakes, and we can correct them, as many of our lawmakers are voted in or out of office by American citizens!

THE WORLD'S FAMOUS ORATIONS

WILLIAM JENNINGS BRYAN
EDITOR-IN-CHIEF

FRANCIS W HALSEY
ASSOCIATE EDITOR

IN TEN VOLUMES

Vol. V
GREAT BRITAIN—III

FUNK and WAGNALLS COMPANY
New York and London

COPYRIGHT, 1906, BY
FUNK & WAGNALLS COMPANY
[Printed in the United States of America]
Published December, 1906

CONTENTS

VOL. V—GREAT BRITAIN—III (1865–1906)

	Page
MACDONALD—On Canadian Confederation (1865)	3
CARLYLE—Address as Lord Rector of Edinburgh University (1866)	17
GOLDWIN SMITH—The Secret Beyond Science	34
BEACONSFIELD—On the Principles of His Party (1872)	38
GLADSTONE—On the Domestic and Foreign Affairs of England (1879)	66
BRADLAUGH—His Plea at the Bar of the House (1881)	91
CHURCHILL—His "Trust the People" Speech (1884)	99
SALISBURY—On the Desertion of Gordon in Egypt (1885)	109
SPURGEON—Men Made Rich by the Poverty of Christ	119
BIRRELL—The Distinction of Burke	131
JAMES BRYCE—On the Government of Ireland Bill (1886)	145
BALFOUR—On the Benefits of Reading (1887)	161

CHAPTER 4

TEXTBOOKS AND CURRICULUM

Out of the ruins of the "crash & burn" rebellion of the 1960's, came some very vocal activists with extreme causes outside of the mainstream of our society. However, they were now armed with tools (new Constitutional laws) for demanding their rights to be heard, and be able to "legally" live outside of the norm, as social deviation was becoming "the norm".

I believe most of us sensed that, because God was no longer in our classrooms, and no longer sanctioned by the U. S. Government, how could He be watching us anywhere else? So why shouldn't we be able do whatever we wanted? And let's not forget the horrific, infamous Manson family cult emerging out of this era, existing on alcohol, drugs, and ritualized Satanistic sexual/murderous acts. Our morals had changed.

We no longer valued life, because we didn't really value monkeys, and they were now our true ancestors under Darwinism, right? So now it was alright to over-medicate, whether or not on Dr. prescribed or over-the-counter advertised "meds", or act out socially/sexually pervasive lifestyles, and fantasies, on the internet, at home, or in public, all under a safe and legal, albeit, immoral blanket. And while most of us chose to sit back complacently, while others made decisions for us (and our children), there continues to be a few, willing to fight for their strange and subversive causes, which if legalized, we must submit to (ourselves and our families).

Although those who protest the loudest for their causes always number in the minority, they tend to bark the loudest and stick with something to the bitter end, as if legalization makes a social or sexual deviation "normal". They persist until their opinions (or life-styles) are either heard and acknowledged, or passed into law, with purposeful intent to twist or warp the Constitution's original meaning. Those causes can be anything from the gay agenda, internet child pornography, terrorist recruitment, abortion, atheism, Satanism, airport Hare Krishna's, etc, etc, which are all protected under various "hate-crime", "free-speech", or "freedom-of- religion" laws. Those causes which might not be as tightly protected, such as the sanctioned removal of our Christian heritage from American and world history, and terrorist recruitment (just to name a few), are now finding a sympathetic ear and a hungry pocket-book at our public colleges, universities, and even within our local primary schools' Boards of Education.

Subversive and pervasive causes which began infiltrating our nation, our laws, and our public schools, with the continuing onslaught of religious-education Supreme Court case rulings, dating back to the 1940's, further sanctioned in the 1960's, continue on today.

When and where is this going to stop? What about the rights of us God-revering, law-abiding, common, yet content folks, who make up the real majority in our nation? Why haven't we put and end to these demeaning and demoralizing behaviors, and public displays of mockery, if not for ourselves, at least for the sakes of our children? If we're not going to take a stand, even for our impressionable children, then we leave ourselves open to every strange influence imaginable, which our kids will encounter, in both the worst and best public school systems.

A re-run of the hit TV series "CSI" (Crime Scene Investigation), airing in January, 2005, had an interesting line, spoken by an actor playing a public high-school counselor, unable to protect her kids from a brutal, school bully's attacks, conceded;

> *"I'm really only able to do something if the kids are*
>
> *called 'faggot' or 'nigger'...*
>
> *but that's about it."*

Unfortunately, this "hands-tied" attitude holds true for many public school campuses, as even the bullies are protected by rights now, as opposed to accountability, under God's Laws, the Ten Commandments. My own son was beat-up, at just six years old, in the first grade after only two weeks attendance at public school. I immediately withdrew him from our "award-winning" school district (national and state-wide recognition), and have been

The Complete Catechism Series
No. 3

A Catechism
OF
Christian Doctrine

Prepared and Enjoined
by order of
The Third Plenary Council of Baltimore

REVISED
by
Rev. M. V. Kelly, C. S. B.

Publishers:
JOHN P. DALEIDEN COMPANY
1530 - 1532 Sedgwick Street,
Chicago, Illinois

PREFACE

All authorities on methods of religious instruction agree on certain fundamental principles:

(1) A catechism is not merely a compendium of theology; it is an attempt to put the truths of religion before the minds of children.

(2) Its language should be directly intelligible to the child, that is to say, the words used should be such as the child already understands, without the aid of glossaries or definitions. One writer on this subject says, "The ideal catechism should contain no definitions and fewer explanations."

(3) The abstract should be avoided. Children speak and are spoken to in the concrete. Our Lord's teaching was in the concrete.

(4) Each question and each answer should contain but one single idea. This is only observing the universally accepted dogma of good teaching—one thing at a time.

(5) As in all good teaching, procedure should be from the known to the unknown.

The Catechism of Christian Doctrine, prepared by the Third Plenary Council of Baltimore, with all its merits, has never claimed to possess these characteristics.

This revision does. It has been prepared solely with the view of presenting all the doctrines enunciated in the original work in the form and according to the methods advocated in schools of catechetics.

To achieve this, certain changes in the order of topics became inevitable but throughout no pains have been spared to treat every item of the subject-matter in full.

Nihil Obstat:
    G. H. MAHOWALD, S. J.,
        Censor Deputatus

Imprimatur:
    ✠ GEORGE CARDINAL MUNDELEIN,
        Archbishop of Chicago.

Copyright, U. S. A., 1929
Printed in U. S. A.

INDEX

END OF MAN	1
GOD	
ANGELS	
ADAM AND EVE	
ORIGINAL SIN	
SIN	
JESUS	
HOLY GHOST	
GRACE	
CHURCH	
INFALLIBILITY	
SACRAMENTS	
BAPTISM	
CONFIRMATION	
CONFESSION	
CONTRITION	54, 58
INDULGENCE	
HOLY EUCHARIST	
COMMUNION	6
MASS	7
EXTREME UNCTION	7
HOLY ORDERS	8
MATRIMONY	85
SACRAMENTALS	8
PRAYER	92
TEN COMMANDMENTS	94
COMMANDMENTS OF THE CHURCH	95-116
LAST JUDGMENT	115
HELL	122
PURGATORY	123
HEAVEN	126

RAUCH & STOECKL PRINTING CO., Inc., 120 ELMWOOD AVE.
BUFFALO, N. Y.

Imprimatur:
    ✠ CHARLES HENRY,
        Bishop of Buffalo

Nihil obstat:
    JOSEPH V. HENNESSEY, D.D.,
        Librorum Censor deputatus

COPYRIGHT 1911
REV. M. PHILLIPS

☞ Only the Answers in heavy print are to be learned by heart

home schooling him ever since, beginning each day with our own morning prayer. Five years ago this became my passionate cause, by which I opened a small private school in one of California's "top/elite" school districts, and became the topic of my Master's thesis.

Other top schools, public and private, from elementary to university, once used the Bible as a textbook, or the main source of, course and textbook content. Such as the early <u>New England Primer</u>, by Dr. Benjamin Rush (1777), a very basic A-B-C approach to spelling, language, poems, songs, Bible verses, prayer, "Duty to God and our Neighbor", the "Golden Rule", "Ten Commandments", and containing various test questions in the back, with the correct (and ethical) answers. Children need to be told what the moral and ethical answers, solutions, and implications are to their problems, until they are old enough, and experienced enough, to formulate these decisions on their own. And as one of our country's first medical doctors, Dr. Rush was a physician as well as one of our nation's Founding Fathers, who also signed the Declaration of Independence in 1776. He was not only interested in but highly dedicated to the formation, implementation and continuation of a public, Biblical-based school system.

Dr. Benjamin Rush also wrote a paper prior to his death (yet wasn't published until 1830, after his death), titled "In Defense of the Use of the Bible in Schools". In this article or "tract" Dr. Rush states what children need to learn,

> "... the great truths of Christianity, before it is preoccupied with less interesting subjects."

His reasoning was children's minds needed to be introduced to great truths, before other nonsense or other "agendas" got in their way. Dr. Rush continued by discussing the sciences, great scientific minds, and religion, pointing out;

> *"The sciences have been compared to a circle, of which religion composes a part. To understand any one of them perfectly, it is necessary to have some knowledge of them all. Bacon, Boyle, and Newton included the Scriptures in the inquiries to which their Universal geniuses disposed them, and their philosophy was aided by their knowledge in them."*

Dr. Rush continues;

> *"I know there is an objection among many people to teaching children doctrines of any kind, because they are liable to be controverted. But let us not be wiser than our Maker. If moral precepts alone could have reformed mankind, the mission of the Son of God into our world would have been unnecessary. He came to promulgate a system of doctrines, as well as a system of morals. The perfect morality of the Gospel rests upon a doctrine which, though often controverted, has never been refuted; . . ."*

Dr. Rush continues by quoting the words of Jesus;

> "... and fixes it upon the eternal and self-moving principle
> of LOVE. It concentrates a whole system of ethics in a single
> text of Scripture:
>
> > 'A new commandment I give unto you, that ye
> > love one another, even as I have loved you.'
>
> By withholding the knowledge of this doctrine from children,
> we deprive ourselves of the best means of awakening moral
> sensibility in their minds. We do more; we furnish an argument
> for withholding from them a knowledge of the morality of the
> Gospel likewise..."

With final comments, Dr. Rush's conclusion;

> "... the universal education of our youth in the principles
> of Christianity by means of the Bible; for this divine book,
> above all others, favors that equality among mankind, that
> respect for just laws, and all those sober and frugal virtues
> which constitute the soul..."

According to Grant Jeffries, author of the book, The Signature of God, and narrative host of the TBN "TV Special" of the same name (2005), he professes (paraphrased);

> "... 87% of all the universities in America started out as Christian Evangelical, with the Bible as the text, such as Harvard University..."

Not only were our nation's first universities Christian schools, but the grade schools and secondary schools were also. This is historically verified by the New England Primer (textbook) by Founding Father Dr. Benjamin Rush, in 1777, our country's first "public" school's Biblically-based text, other than the Bible. The Bible was reserved for college-level studies, and the historical facts presented within the pages of the Bible were studied as factual, long before it's historical verification by the discovery of the Dead Sea scrolls, or Noah's Ark found on Mt. Ararat, Turkey. And without trying to make a case for, or against the Bible's undisputable validity, the fact the Bible was used as an early textbook in our country's schools, confirms our early nation's Christian heritage.

However, there are now well-meaning organizations which insure the "political correctness" of our children's elementary through high school texts, by perusing them for any mention of our Founding Father's religious (Christian) affiliations, holidays, etc. These sensitive, albeit documented "historic" issues, have been purposefully deleted from our children's textbooks, and our nation's historic beginnings. In a true Christian "spirit" of not wanting to offend

A DEFENCE OF THE USE OF THE BIBLE IN SCHOOLS

By Dr. Benjamin Rush **(1745-1813), distinguished physician and signer of the Declaration of Independence in 1776.**

Benjamin Rush's 1830 tract

Dr. Rush was an outspoken Christian, statesman, and pioneering medical doctor. He was a prolific author, publishing the first American chemistry textbook. In 1797, President John Adams appointed Rush as Treasurer of the U.S. Mint, a position he held until 1813. He also founded America's first Bible society. At the time of his death in 1813, he was heralded as one of the three most notable figures of America, the other two being George Washington and Benjamin Franklin.

Dear Sir:

It is now several months since I promised to give you my reasons for preferring the Bible as a schoolbook to all other compositions. Before I state my arguments, I shall assume the five following propositions:

> 1. That Christianity is the only true and perfect religion; and that in proportion as mankind adopt its principles and obey its precepts they will be wise and happy.
>
> 2. That a better knowledge of this religion is to be acquired by reading the Bible than in any other way.
>
> 3. That the Bible contains more knowledge necessary to man in his present state than any other book in the world.
>
> 4. That knowledge is most durable, and religious instruction most useful, when imparted in early life.

anyone, we have changed our country's history, and this is the educational legacy we are passing down to our children. I have one of my mom's original public school primers from 1931, A Book of Famous Poems, which includes lessons, songs like "Battle-Hymn of the Republic" (mentioning both God and Christ), poems and Bible passages such as the 23rd Psalm and the Beatitudes; remember this was the same year the Supreme Court declared (one of the last times), *"We are a Christian people . . .".*

We have replaced the public school curriculum of teaching values, morals, language, arithmetic, and history (as it actually occurred); with everything from social-sex education, promoting "alternative" lifestyles; tolerance for all faiths (irregardless of their support of terrorism or Satanism); and cramming higher mathematics down the throats of our youngest grade-schoolers. This is an attempt to compensate academically for our country's decaying morals, and the enormous void left by wiping God off our educational slate.

There is a growing trend among University professors who are now "in-the-business" of authoring their own curriculum/course textbooks, using them as a forum for their own personal; political, sexual, or prejudicial agendas and biases. One such American History Professor/author was recently interviewed on a television news program where he indicated his own bias against the Christian faith, and did not think that our nation's Founding Fathers were actually Christian, nor did he believe our country began with Judeo-Christianity at it's roots (albeit recorded documentation in the Preamble to the Constitution, Declaration of Independence, etc.). This U.C.L.A. (University of California at Los Angeles) history professor admittedly rewrote history leaving out all references to our Christian beginnings within his textbook AND the university course. Is it legal to rewrite history, according to one's own beliefs? Is it legal to force students to purchase historically and factually incorrect textbooks for mandatory curriculum based on half-truths?

Additionally, teaching our elementary school children about sex in "sex-education" classes was not mandated in any Preamble or Constitutional Amendment I read. However a portion of the Declaration of Independence does state;

> *"We hold these truths to be self-evident,*
>
> *that all men are created equal,*
>
> *that they are endowed by their Creator with certain*
>
> *unalienable Rights,*
>
> *that among these are Life, Liberty and the*
>
> *pursuit of Happiness."*

Maybe the *"pursuit of Happiness"* is misinterpreted to mean pursuing "fun" instead of fulfillment, and though I will be discussing the Constitution and Declaration of Independence more in the following chapters, it would appear that the above stated phrases have been erroneously translated by our school districts and courts to justify removing Christian Religious Ed classes and replacing them with "sex-ed" classes, with sexually explicit textbooks. Sadly, we have been (unknowingly) allowing our teachers to present their own unbridled personal ideals, preferences, perversions, and agendas to our children, without merit and are disciplined only when; a.) they get caught or, b.) they teach anything from a documented Christian perspective, or Judeo-Christian Biblical world view.

Universities as well as primary school districts are refusing to include Christian religious inferences, in their coursework and textbooks, denying our children the truth of who we are as a nation, as a people. Concurrently, there are also Intelligent Design verses Darwinism/ Evolution/Origin of Species battles in our departments of education, universities, lower and higher courts, and finally represented on the movie screens.

Not since his brief appearances in the 1980's, "brat-pack" movies-gone-to-school classic, "Ferris Bueller's Day Off" (teens ditching a day of meaningless public school), portraying a teacher; or giving more chalkboard instruction about *"red-dry-eyes"* in Visine Eye Drops commercials has actor-producer-intellectual, Ben Stein been so true to form as he is in his new documentary and "call-to-action" movie, "Expelled, No Intelligence Allowed", from Premise Media Corp., 2008.

The movie "Expelled, No Intelligence Allowed" exposes many in the academic, legal, and scientific communities, who claim Creationism or Intelligent Design infers a "Creator" or deity, therefore making it non-academic, unscientific, religious dogma; and quoting the high court ruling stated in an earlier chapter, *". . . is unconstitutional, therefore illegal"* (?) Unfortunately professional chastisement and career annihilation is now attached to teaching the "other" widely-held theory of our origins; Creationism or Intelligent Design (as clearly defined in the Bible, the Torah, and other faith-based doctrines). A Harris Poll taken in July, 2005, found that 82 percent of those surveyed believed that other theories, such as Biblical Creationism and Intelligent Design should be taught in schools. Only 12 percent believed that evolution should be the only theory taught. Even William F. Buckley, Jr., intellectual, T.V. journalistic/host, and former editor of the "New Yorker" magazine, took a jab at the self-proclaimed "naturalist's theories or beliefs, by suggesting we give credit where credit is due when he stated;

> *"This I believe:*
>
> > *that it is intellectually easier to credit*
> > *a divine intelligence than to submit*
> > *dumbly to felicitous congeries about nature."*

If in fact Christian views are deemed or sanctioned unconstitutional, and we're not allowed to teach it to our children in public (government) schools, yet we are forced to teach cultural sensitivity (to desensitize our young to politically-correct politeness towards other, "terrorist-based" faiths, or "unusual", sexual preferences or practices, albeit legal or illegal) from a very young age and more specifically to our babies and toddlers in government and/or publicly-funded preschools, as curriculum; then we are merely promoting atheistic Communism, Socialism, Planned Parenthood infanticide, or Nazism genocide; and have indeed reverted backwards to a dangerously simple-minded, prejudicial, and unintelligible society.

One Hundred and One Famous Poems

Revised Edition

With a
Prose Supplement

COPYRIGHT 1924
R. J. COOK
391 So. Warsaw Ave.
CHICAGO

Executive Mansion
Washington, Nov 21, 1864

To Mrs. Bixby, Boston, Mass.
Dear Madam:—

I have been shown in the files of the War Department a statement of the Adjutant General of Massachusetts that you are the mother of five sons who died gloriously on the field of battle. I feel how weak and fruitless must be any word of mine which should attempt to beguile you from the grief of a loss so overwhelming. But I cannot refrain from tendering you the consolation that may be found in the thanks of the republic they died to save. I pray that our Heavenly Father may assuage the anguish of your bereavement, and leave you only the cherished memory of the loved and lost, and the solemn pride that must be yours to have laid so costly a sacrifice upon the altar of freedom.

Yours very sincerely and respectfully,
A. Lincoln.

On the walls of Brasenose College, Oxford University, England, this letter of the "rail-splitter" President hangs as a model of purest English, rarely, if ever, surpassed.

The Ten Commandments

I

I am the Lord thy God, which have brought thee out the land of Egypt, out of the house of bondage.

Thou shalt have no other gods before me.

II

Thou shalt not make unto thee any graven image, or any likeness of any thing that is in heaven above, or that is in the earth beneath, or that is in the water under the earth:

Thou shalt not bow down thyself to them, nor serve them: for I the Lord thy God am a jealous God, visiting the iniquity of the fathers upon the children unto the third and fourth generation of them that hate me;

And shewing mercy unto thousands of them that love me, and keep my commandments.

III

Thou shalt not take the name of the Lord thy God in vain; for the Lord will not hold him guiltless that taketh his name in vain.

IV

Remember the Sabbath day to keep it holy:

Six days shalt thou labor and do all thy work:

But the seventh day is the Sabbath of the Lord thy God; in it thou shalt not do any work, thou, nor thy son, nor thy daughter, thy man-servant, nor thy maid-servant, nor thy cattle, nor the stranger that is within thy gates:

For in six days the Lord made heaven and earth, the sea, and all that in them is, and rested the seventh day: wherefore the Lord blessed the Sabbath day, and hallowed it.

V

Honour thy father and thy mother: that thy days may be long upon the land which the Lord thy God giveth thee.

VI

Thou shalt not kill.

VII

Thou shalt not commit adultery.

VIII

Thou shalt not steal.

IX

Thou shalt not bear false witness against thy neighbor.

X

Thou shalt not covet thy neighbor's house, thou shalt not covet thy neighbor's wife, nor his man-servant, nor his maid-servant, nor his ox, nor his ass, nor any thing that is thy neighbor's.

✧ ✧ ✧

Magna Charta

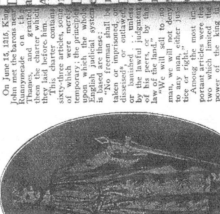

On June 15, 1215, King John met the barons near Runnymeade on the Thames, and granted them the charter which they laid before him.

This charter contains sixty-three articles, some of which were merely temporary; the principles upon which the whole English judicial system is based are these:

"No freeman shall be taken or imprisoned, or disseised*, or outlawed or banished . . . unless by the lawful judgment of his peers, or by the law of the land."

"We will sell to no man, we will not deny to any man, either justice or right."

Among the most important articles were the two which limited the power of the king in matters of taxation:

"No scutage or aid shall be imposed in our kingdom unless by the general council of our kingdom," and

"For the holding of the general council of the kingdom, we shall cause to be summoned the archbishops, abbots, earls, and the greater barons of the realm, singly, by our letters. And furthermore we shall cause to be summoned generally by our sheriffs and bailiffs, all others who hold of us in chief."

—Engraved for Sydney's "History of England"

*Dispossessed of land.

ON choosing books for children these rules, recently laid down by an author of books for boys, are worth the consideration of parents:

"Read your children's books yourself. Or better still, get your boy or girl to read them aloud to you. Ask yourself during the reading:

Does this book lay stress on villainy, deception or treachery?

Are all the incidents wholesome, probable and true to life?

Does it show young people contemptuous toward their elders and successfully opposing them?

Do the young characters in the book show respect for teachers and others in authority?

Are these characters the kind of young people you wish your children to associate with?

Does the book speak of and describe pranks, practical jokes and pieces of thoughtless and cruel mischief as though they were funny and worthy of imitation?

Is the English good and is the story written in good style?"

CHATER 5

SYMBOLS AND RULINGS

Unfortunately the deterioration of our society, our economy, and academic content within our higher-learning institutions rides on the heels of removing God and our Christian heritage, not only from our schools, but our country, and our lives. This has been happening state by state throughout the United States.

The states of Massachusetts and California are the first two states to recognize and sanction a non-Biblical marriage union between two same-sexed individuals, and the rest of us didn't want to know about it. I don't want to know your sexual preferences, and you don't want to know mine. Well we didn't want to know about theirs either, and unfortunately theirs has been blasting non-stop on every local and national television news station since legislation was enacted. We've seen enough! What exactly is the purpose of interrupting children's T.V. programs to report this "breaking news"? For the sake of indoctrinating our children? How did you explain this anomaly to your kids?

The state of California has become notorious for its "free thinkers" (and doers), politically liberal and socially aloof/independent, however our state's court ruled against the popular vote, the majority, and we are currently petitioning to get this "off the books". Can't we just

From this: L.A. County Seal

notice cross

DEPARTMEN

PATRICIA PLOEHN
Director

To this:

208

cross missing

Los Ang

Us

An

A Whole Family Foster Ho
trained to assist the

A Shared Responsibili

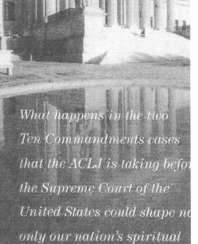

It Does Matter

*What happens in the two Ten Commandments cases that the ACLJ is taking befor the Supreme Court of the United States could shape n only our nation's spiritual landscape — but **your personal freedom to share or express your faith.***

keep sexuality a personal and private matter? Shamefully, we've allowed the courts to rewrite the Constitution for us, and with that, removing all nuances, traditions, statues, and symbols representing God and Christianity from our life and civilization completely, filling the void with non-acceptable T.V. viewing for our kids, unable to escape the "news".

Unfortunately, liberated California is not the only state ignoring our country's documented Christian heritage, or ruling against majority voters; while placating the gay, the atheist, the terrorist, and we shouldn't be happy about that behavior, whether from federal or state "elected" officials or judges! And these days merely the "threat" of a law-suit is enough to remove the crosses from the city logo in Las Cruces (Spanish for crosses), New Mexico, and the official seal of the County of Los Angeles (Spanish for angels), California. And worse, The Ten Commandments (God's laws) are also being attacked by law suits, and removed from courthouses, schools and official buildings throughout the U.S. These ten simple laws are the very basis for the establishment of our governing bodies and those carved-in-stone Commandments are: (reprinted from ADF "Alliance Defense Fund" brochure)

1. **"You shall have no other Gods before me"**

   "The presupposition for American liberty is the belief that liberty itself is a gift from God. Nearly every state constitution has a mention or recognition, of the existence of God or a Supreme Being."

2. "You shall not make for yourself an idol in the form of anything in heaven above or on the earth beneath or in the water below. You shall not bow down to them or worship them . . ."

3. "You shall not misuse the name of the Lord your God, for the Lord will not hold anyone guiltless who misuses his name."

4. "Remember the Sabbath Day by keeping it holy."

    "In 1961, the United States Supreme Court upheld the constitutionality of Sabbath laws. There have been many valid secular reasons as well for honoring the Sabbath as a day of rest. Following the commandment's principles, numerous labor laws have been passed to limit the number of hours required of workers in a week. Many state courts have ruled that it is appropriate for states to impose Sunday restrictions for the purpose of promoting public health, safety, general welfare, and morals."

5. "Honor your father and mother . . ."

    "Strong families are basic for social order in both secular and faith-based societies. Numerous studies from respected academics have documented that when the family breaks down, and along with it parental authority, the consequences for the future of society are largely negative."

6. "You shall not murder."

7. "You shall not commit adultery."

> "... adultery laws help protect each of the spouses, the family, children, and the secular social order."

8. "You shall not steal."

9. "You shall not give false testimony against your neighbor."

> "This commandment is the foundation of our nation's judicial system. Anyone who testifies in a court of law must agree to an oath that he or she will tell the truth or face the criminal penalty of perjury. The criminal penalties against perjury remain steep in many states and, in some cases, states are trying to increase the criminal penalty for lying under oath."

10. "You shall not covet ..."

> "... this commandment has been cited as the basis for civil laws against election fraud and white collar crime."

The ADF brochure on the Ten Commandments summarizes;

> *"To deny the role that the Ten Commandments have played in the development of our nation's laws and jurisprudence is to deny the very foundations upon which our nation is based. If we forget our moral foundation, then all other aspects of a free and democratic society will come tumbling down. In addition, the respect for all law weakens - resulting in social anarchy - and a far more dangerous place to live."*

> *"That is why the Ten Commandments must be viewed as an historical document upon which almost all of American jurisprudence is based - and not an unconstitutional establishment of religion, as the ACLU and its allies strongly contend."*

Quoting former President Harry S. Truman, on his thoughts regarding God's Ten Commandments (echoed over and over by most U.S. Presidents);

> *"The fundamental basis of this nation's laws was given to Moses on the Mount. The fundamental basis of our Bill of Rights comes from the teachings . . . If we don't have the proper fundamental moral background, we will finally wind up with a totalitarian government which does not believe in rights for anybody except the state."*

Regretfully, lawsuits brought on by the American Civil Liberties Union (ACLU) has, and could force the future removal of the Ten Commandments displayed in over 4,000 different school, court house, and public square locations throughout America. And again quoting the Alliance Defense Fund, a news article titled, "Banning the Ten Commandments";

> "In addition to filing lawsuits to force the removal of the Ten Commandments, the ACLU:
>
> - Pushes same-sex "marriage" and much more of the homosexual legal agenda
>
> - Works to prevent Christians and ministries from publicly sharing the Gospel at various times and places
>
> - <u>Defends</u> the distribution of child pornography and files lawsuits <u>against</u> laws to protect children from registered sex offenders"

The American Defense Fund poses the question what will happen if the ACLU is ultimately victorious in their quest, and what the consequences could be when questioning;

> "If the ACLU eventually wins a U.S. Supreme Court case that bans the display of religious language on government property, even historically significant inscriptions like Abraham Lincoln's Second Inaugural Address at the Lincoln Memorial in Washington, D.C., with its many allusions to God and Scripture, could be "edited" to remove those 'offensive' words."

Banning the Ten Commandments

Recent Supreme Court rulings on the constitutionality of public Ten Commandments displays have conservative and liberal legal organizations preparing for a series of critical battles.

Conservative legal experts are expressing grave concern about the wave of lawsuits being filed by the American Civil Liberties Union (ACLU) and its allies challenging the constitutionality of Ten Commandments and similar faith/history displays on public property.

Decisions by the sharply divided Supreme Court in June 2005 have only added fuel to the fire—some monuments have been ruled constitutional, while others have been banned. The High Court seems to have sent the message that— for now—many cases on Ten Commandments displays will be decided one by one.

And the ACLU, America's number-one religious censor, with a war chest of over $175 million and its army of more than 2,000 allied lawyers, is only too happy to oblige.

Because each ACLU lawsuit can censor another piece of America's Judeo-Christian history and heritage, while its loss simply protects the status quo—for now—the ACLU and its allies' increasingly aggressive litigious "search and destroy" mission continues to inflict damage on religious liberty.

One High Court showdown—*McCreary County v. ACLU*—led to the forced removal of a Ten Commandments display at the McCreary County, Kentucky, courthouse.

And in Georgia, a U.S. district court judge ordered a Habersham County courthouse to remove every public display of the Ten Commandments after a two-year legal battle with the ACLU.

These attacks portend a high-stakes showdown that could ultimately lead to a U.S. Supreme Court ruling fully banning the Ten Commandments, along with other religiously themed displays across the nation.

However, the ACLU isn't invincible. It has lost key battles, including the *Van Orden v. Perry* Supreme Court decision in June 2005. In that case, the Court rejected demands by a group of atheists to remove a display of the Ten Commandments on the Texas State Capitol building. It also lost at the U.S. Court of Appeals for the Sixth Circuit in December 2005 in a case (at the lower court level) involving a display in Mercer County, Kentucky. That court wrote, *"The ACLU's argument contains ... fundamental flaws. First, the ACLU makes repeated reference to 'the separation of church and state.' This extra-constitutional construct has grown tiresome. The First Amendment does not demand a wall of separation between church and state."*

In an earlier high-profile case, the ACLU filed a lawsuit on behalf of the Freethought Society of Greater Philadelphia.

Members of this atheist group said they were "offended" by a plaque of the Ten Commandments

State Rep. Elinor Z. Taylor, of West Chester, Pa., placed flowers by a newly covered Ten Commandments plaque on the Chester County Courthouse after a judge ruled for the ACLU and ordered the plaque temporarily shrouded pending an appeal. When the county won its appeal, the shroud was removed. But if the ACLU presses its demands, the Ten Commandments plaque again could be in jeopardy as are many such expressions of America's Christian heritage across the nation.

on the exterior wall of the Chester County Courthouse, which had been there continually since 1920.

In the first round, U.S. District Judge Stewart Dalzell ruled for the ACLU and the atheists. The judge said that posting a religious document on a courthouse was a government endorsement of a particular religion, which he said is forbidden by the First Amendment. A federal appeals court then reversed this ruling and ruled the Ten Commandments plaque could stay.

But it's what happened after the initial ruling in this case that provides a glimpse of what will transpire across the country if the ACLU is allowed to ultimately win its war against the Ten Commandments and America's Christian heritage. After the federal district court judge ruled for the ACLU, he said the 50-by-39-inch bronze plaque must be covered pending an appeals court ruling. When workers placed a plastic shroud over the plaque in 2002, more than 100 people gathered to pray and peacefully protest.

"Imagine if across America every plaque like this that represents our nation's heritage were covered or removed," says Alan Sears, president and general counsel of the Alliance Defense Fund (ADF). The Alliance is a Scottsdale, Arizona–based Christian legal group that frequently battles the ACLU over public displays of the Ten Commandments, and it has played a key role through strategy, training, funding, and/or direct litigation in several important victories over the ACLU, including the previously mentioned *Van Orden v. Perry* Supreme Court decision this past June and the *American Civil Liberties Union v. Mercer County, Kentucky* case in December.

Sears continues, "It could happen. And people who care about religious liberty and preserving our nation's heritage should be alarmed. Although the Pennsylvania case has been resolved and the Ten Commandments have been uncovered, this kind of legal harassment and intimidation by the ACLU represents just the tip of the iceberg and part of a growing hostility to America's Christian heritage."

The Alliance was founded in 1994 by Dr. James Dobson, Dr. D. James Kennedy, the late Dr. Bill Bright and the late Larry Burkett, and other evangelical leaders.

According to public records, approximately 19 disputes involving the public posting of the Ten Commandments are pending across the nation. While no single case is expected to decisively settle the issue, each one can either enhance religious freedom or religious censorship.

That's why ADF is unyielding in its opposition to the ACLU and its allies. ADF is meeting the ACLU head-on throughout the country in one high-stakes showdown after another— including in Arizona, where the ACLU demanded the removal of a Ten Commandments monument

(continued on back)

> "The ACLU aims to secure a U.S. Supreme Court decision that bans not only the Ten Commandments, but virtually every historic religious display on *all* government property everywhere."

Banning the Ten Commandments
(continued from front)

from a Phoenix park. The monument—virtually identical to the one at the Texas State Capitol that was declared constitutional this past June by the U.S. Supreme Court—is one of 20 similar memorials in the park that celebrate Arizona's history and culture.

The Alliance is helping oppose the ACLU and its allies in this and a growing number of other cases.

Sears, who prior to heading the Alliance was a highly regarded federal prosecutor in the U.S. Department of Justice and executive director of the Attorney General's Commission on Pornography during the Reagan administration, says, "The ACLU aims to secure a U.S. Supreme Court decision that bans not only the Ten Commandments, but virtually every historic religious display on *all* government property *everywhere*."

Sears passionately argues, "People are kidding themselves if they think this could never happen. It can happen here. The ACLU *wants it* to happen, and with its tens of millions of dollars in resources, it is pursuing that ultimate goal."

"Displays like the Ten Commandments tell a critically important part of America's history," explains Sears. "They make it clear that America is not like other nations. Much of our legal system was deliberately established on principles derived directly from the Bible. In fact, 12 of the original 13 colonies incorporated the entire Ten Commandments into their civil and criminal laws."

The implications are staggering for places like Washington, D.C., which contains thousands of Christian and Jewish inscriptions on public buildings and monuments.

Sears says that if the ACLU gets its way, every one of these displays will have to be removed or altered in some way to "edit" the "offending" words and images.

"The bad news," stresses Sears, "is that if God's people don't respond adequately, the ACLU is dangerously close—far closer than almost anyone realizes—to cleansing America's public recognition of its historic Christian roots."

Thankfully, the Alliance has already helped win a growing number of notable cases, including the *Van Orden v. Perry* Supreme Court victory and federal appeals court decisions allowing Ten Commandments monuments to remain at the Chester County, Pennsylvania, and Mercer County, Kentucky, courthouses.

But despite these significant successes—and many others not mentioned here—the Alliance Defense Fund and its allies still lag far behind the ACLU in resources on this and many other issues.

That is why the Alliance Defense Fund has launched the National Campaign to Stop the American Civil Liberties Union. Sears hopes many Christians will send a tax-deductible contribution to help the Alliance defend the Ten Commandments and other displays of America's heritage and to help defeat the ACLU and its plans on many other fronts.

In addition to filing lawsuits to force the removal of the Ten Commandments, the ACLU:
- Pushes same-sex "marriage" and much more of the homosexual legal agenda
- Works to prevent Christians and ministries from publicly sharing the Gospel at various times and places
- Defends the distribution of child pornography and files lawsuits against laws to protect children from registered sex offenders

But Sears knows the ACLU can be stopped. In the past decade, the Alliance Defense Fund and its allies have won nearly three out of four of the hundreds of cases funded and litigated to a conclusion. These victories have helped secure

If the ACLU eventually wins a U.S. Supreme Court case that bans the display of religious language on government property, even historically significant inscriptions like Abraham Lincoln's Second Inaugural Address at the Lincoln Memorial in Washington, D.C., with its many allusions to God and Scripture, could be "edited" to remove those "offensive" words.

protections for family values, religious freedom, and the sanctity of human life. The Alliance Defense Fund has also had a part in 26 U.S. Supreme Court victories.

In clashes with the ACLU, ADF-backed attorneys have an impressive track record, including their efforts in *Dale v. Boy Scouts of America*, in which the ACLU lost its bid to force the Boy Scouts of America to accept homosexual scout leaders.

Even though it appears that, by God's grace, the ACLU has finally met its match, many observers believe that this group, which began early last century to advance a radical secular and anti-Christian cause, has already done grave damage to our country.

Now, with its allies, the ACLU continues to attack any public expression of the Christian faith or Judeo-Christian teachings, such as the Ten Commandments.

Sears reiterates his point that, as anyone who follows the news knows, "the ACLU is dramatically stepping up its offensive in what clearly is a huge push for the big prize: a series of landmark Supreme Court rulings that would purge many forms of religious expression from the 'public square.'"

Sears says the reason he hopes many Christians will contribute generously to the Alliance for the Ten Commandments and many other winnable battles is this: "If the ACLU can successfully purge symbols and words such as the Ten Commandments from our public life, who is to say *your* words, *your* speech, *your* expression of *your* faith can't ultimately be denied?"

"I hope every person who understands the grave threat that the ACLU poses to their freedoms will send a generous tax-deductible gift today to support the Alliance's National Campaign to Stop the ACLU," says Sears, "because the destruction of America's heritage that our opponents have in mind will only lead to chaos and darkness."

According to Sears, donor contributions will help support the Alliance Defense Fund's fourfold mission:

1. **Provide funds** to help allied attorneys litigate and defeat the ACLU and its allies in precedent-setting legal cases involving family values, religious freedom, and the sanctity of human life.
2. **Litigate cases** to keep ADF in the battle defending your freedoms and values.
3. **Train attorneys** in the best tactics and strategies to defeat the ACLU and its allies. Through its one-of-a-kind National Litigation Academy℠, ADF is working toward a goal of training 5,000 allied attorneys to fight—and win—for Christian values in America's courtrooms.
4. **Strategize and coordinate** the efforts of many legal groups that share the same values to oppose the ACLU and its allies.

"More specifically," explains Sears, "if we can raise critical funds in the next 60 days, we can unleash more and more resources needed to defeat the ACLU in its war on America's Christian heritage."

Sears emphatically believes that "with God's grace, the ADF-backed attorneys can win. But they need prayers and support to stay in the fight all the way to the end."

He drives his point home: "We can take America's law back from the radicals. We can keep our country safe for our children and grandchildren. We can guard religious freedom against attacks by extremists who aim to silence us for our religious faith and conduct. But the only way we can raise the money for our fight against the ACLU is with the immediate prayers and help of people who share our concern over the ACLU's radical attacks on America's Christian heritage."

The Alliance Defense Fund is completely cash based. ADF never borrows money or steps into a new legal battle "on faith in humans," hoping the funds will come in later. That means when people contribute, they will never receive "crisis" appeals begging for money to erase a budget deficit.

Sears says, "If God's people give us adequate funding, which He always has ensured, we move forward. If not, we don't. We are totally dependent on the Lord to move the hearts of people to help us."

To support ADF's National Campaign to Stop the ACLU and its attacks on America's bedrock values, tax-deductible contributions can be sent to:

Alan E. Sears
President, CEO & General Counsel
Alliance Defense Fund
15333 N. Pima Road, Suite 165
Scottsdale, AZ 85260

Within virtually every U.S. state's individual constitution or bylaws the Ten Commandments and/or God have been referenced in one way or another, and would appear to be the only True moral code of our land. This public expression of our Christian faith is reiterated by our National Motto:

"In God We Trust".

This reverent phrase became our national motto in 1956, one year after Congress mandated the phrase to be printed on all our coins and every denomination of paper bills, in 1955. This was initiated in 1864, during the Civil War, when *"In God We Trust"* first appeared on the two-cent coin. Under God's protection, we have become the wealthiest nation in the world, with seemingly unlimited resources to help many other third-world nations. And now our National Motto is in danger of being removed from our money as well as *"under God"* from the Pledge of Allegiance, and along with it, every national monument in Washington D.C.

The one single driving force behind this move to get God off our coins and out of the Pledge of Allegiance is an atheist named Michael Newdow, who has been fighting this in the courts for many years now. Tracking his pathetic plight on the nightly news, he began claiming that his daughter (whom he lost custody of or visitation rights to after a messy divorce), was being forced to acknowledge God as part of her Pledge of Allegiance, and that it offended him (not her). According to "Impact Newsletter" the February, 2006, issue titled "Newdow Attacks 'In God We Trust'" (I paraphrase), Mr. Newdow was an emergency room technician with a

CORAL RIDGE MINISTRIES

IN GOD WE TRUST:

A BRIEF HISTORY

In the early days of the Civil War, Treasury Secretary Salmon P. Chase instructed the director of the U.S. mint at Philadelphia to prepare a motto for the nation's coins:

"Dear Sir," his memo began: "No nation can be strong except in the strength of God, or safe except in His defense. The trust of our people in God should be declared on our national coins."

(over)

After a few options were considered, Chase settled on IN GOD WE TRUST; Congress passed the necessary legislation, and the motto first appeared on the 1864 two-cent coin.

IN GOD WE TRUST has been in continuous use on the penny since 1909, and on the dime coin since 1916.

In fact, since 1938, all United States coins have borne the inscription.

(When the motto was left off of a new double-eagle gold coin in 1907, the public's outcry led Congress to order it restored.)

In 1956, the Congress and President Eisenhower agreed to declare IN GOD WE TRUST the "national motto of the United States."

The motto then began to appear on our paper money also.

© 2006 Coral Ridge Ministries Media, Inc.
All Rights Reserved
www.coralridge.org

to eliminate any public reference to God from our national landscape.) Court briefs are due this month.

law degree, and has also founded his own atheistic "church", the First Amendmist Church of True Science, and appointed himself "Grand Lubitz". (Whatever that is?!) This article continues, and I now quote;

> "Newdow charges in his brief that it is 'deeply offensive' for the government to advocate what he 'specifically decries'. Not only is he offended, he alleges a long list of other grievances in his suit. The motto turns him into a 'political outsider', forces him to pay tax dollars for a religious notion, infringes his right to exercise his Religion, and violates his rights under the Religious Freedom Restoration Act, as well as his free speech and equal protection rights."

The article closes with the results of a Fox News poll taken in November 2005;

> "81 percent of Americans disagree with the statement that religion should be 'excluded from public life'. Some 90 percent want 'under God' kept in the Pledge of Allegiance and 93 percent want to keep 'In God We Trust' on our monies."

Hopefully the courts will side with the popular vote, the American people they are supposed to be representing in these matters, and not try to rewrite the Constitution, or the First Amendment to appease one broken "squeaky" wheel.

Eluding to our National Motto almost 140 years before an act of Congress made it so, Francis Scott Key wrote our National Anthem, "The Star Spangled Banner" in 1814, and in the fourth stanza it states,

> *"And this be our motto,*
>
> *In God is our Trust".*

Today, we face loosing our beloved National Motto and our Christian roots in American history, just as we lost our freedom to pray and have Bible study in public schools in the 1960's. Regarding our National Motto, Chief Counsel for the American Center for Law and Justice (ACLJ), Jay Sekulow states,

> *"The underlying premise of the National Motto can be traced to our founding. The Declaration of Independence says that we are endowed by our Creator with certain unalienable rights. The founders recognized that rights and liberties are derived from an authority higher than government, which means that government cannot take these rights and liberties away."*

And although retired Supreme Court Justice Sandra Day O'Connor tended to flip-flop on most religious issues, arguing on one hand that the phrase *"under God",*

> *". . . has long since lost meaning, and is not to be taken literally."*

Justice O'Connor also reiterated the same sentiments of the American Center for Law and Justice, while addressing the constitutionality of a 2004, Pledge of Allegiance case, eloquently stating;

> *"It is unsurprising that a nation founded by religious refugees and dedicated to religious freedom should find references to divinity in its symbols, songs, mottoes and oaths. Eradicating such references would sever ties to a history that sustains this Nation even today."*

PART II

COLONIZATION

&

FOUNDING DOCUMENTS

"The rights of man come not from

the generosity of the state

but from the hand of God."

-John Fitzgerald Kennedy

(35th President, J.F.K.)

CHAPTER 6

CONSTITUTION & DECLARATION

June, 1776, the Second Continental Congress met and appointed a committee of five statesmen to write a declaration freeing the thirteen colonies from British rule. Those five men were: John Adams, Benjamin Franklin, Thomas Jefferson, Robert Livingston, and Roger Sherman, who wrote "The unanimous Declaration (of Independence) of the thirteen united States of America" (the actual original title given to the Declaration of Independence), proclaimed on July 4, 1776. This founding document clearly makes references to the "unanimous" religious beliefs of the people, as represented in these passages:

> *"When in the Course of human events, it becomes necessary . . . the separate and equal station to which the Laws of Nature and of nature's God entitle them . . .*
>
> *We hold these truths to be self-evident, that all men are created equal, that they are endowed by their Creator with certain unalienable Rights, that among these are Life, Liberty . . .*
>
> *We, therefore, . . . appealing to the Supreme Judge of the world for the rectitude of our intentions . . ."*

> *"And for the support of this Declaration, with a firm reliance on the protection of divine Providence, we mutually pledge to each other our Lives, our fortunes and our sacred Honor."*

In this Declaration, references to God are clear; *"God"*, *"their Creator"*, *"Supreme Judge of the world"*. However the phrase which might not stand out, yet truly references the religious climate, of our founding heritage based upon belief in God is;

> *"with a firm reliance on the protection of divine Providence, we mutually pledge . . .".*

Essentially meaning *"in God we trust"*, and we're back to our National Motto.

Julia Duin of the "Washington Times" concurs, as in her April 13, 2005, article titled "Religion Under a Secular Assault", when she states;

> *"The Declaration of Independence acknowledged the Judeo-Christian deity in appealing to 'Nature's God', 'Divine Providence' and 'the Supreme Judge of the world'".*

And another point she made in this article, regarding the Ten Commandments and the First Amendment to the Constitution was;

"Though many Americans cannot recite the Ten Commandments . . . an Associated Press survey in February (2005) found that 76 percent of the 1,000 people polled approved of displaying them on government property. . . . Opponents say such displays violate the establishment clause of the First Amendment to the Constitution: 'Congress shall make no law respecting an establishment of religion or prohibiting the free exercise thereof'. . . . The intent, scholars say, was to protect Americans from an imposed state religion, guaranteeing the right to worship God however they pleased."

Former Speaker of the House Newt Gingrich, recently wrote an "interactive" book titled Rediscovering God in America, "Reflections on the Role of Faith in Our Nation's History and Future", 2006. An interactive historic walk-through tour guide, to many of our National Treasures consisting of, architecture, documents, memorials, and monuments throughout Washington D.C., most of which carry references to God, and/or prayer, the Bible, the Gospel, Christianity, etc.

The inside cover sleeve of this book contains an invitation from Former Speaker Gingrich, encouraging everyone to tour America's capital city he says,

"This walking tour is not just a look at the architecture and beauty of our nation's capitol; it is a tour of American history, of the great men and women, the great events, the great documents and great"

> *"institutions, the great ideas - all shaped decisively by the genuine belief that we are a nation under God - that are at the heart of our freedom as Americans and our identity as a people."*

Mr. Gingrich continues to make the case for our Christian heritage, and only solution for our future, when he concludes,

> *"The next time a friend or colleague says that religious expression has no place in the public square and that discussion of God has no place in our children's history and government classes, you will only need to tell them about what you experienced on this simple walk to remind them of God's role in America's history - and America's future. Your friend,*
>
> *Newt Gingrich"*

How is it possible that with the enormous wealth of resources and authenticated historical documentation available throughout our nation that anyone could confuse our Judeo-Christian heritage for anything less? Why are other faiths, or the believers in no faith at all (atheism) so threatened at the prospect of acknowledging our nation's true Christian founding roots; in the very nation that they are Constitutionally free/first amendment free (not forced) to practice their own beliefs in? It appears many U.S. citizens suffer from a debilitating form of either denial, or sheer ignorance.

—that the government of the people, by the people, for the people, shall not perish from the earth.

Despite all the unmistakable and irrefutable documentation and monumentation (my own descriptive word for set-in-stone writs on national monuments) planted throughout our country, in our capitol district of Washington D.C., at Independence Hall in Philadelphia, Pennsylvania, or Boston, Massachusetts, etc. regarding our Judeo-Christian heritage, as posed on the website UnderGodProCon.org, it would seem the big question/confusion these days is:

"Was the U.S. founded 'under God'?"

An impartial balance-sheet style (pro/yes, con/no) answer for this absurd question is aptly addressed for those too blind to see, too lazy to research, too ignorant, or illiterate to care what the truth really is, and as expected the "pro/yes" column out-weighs the "con/no" column. Unfortunately, and without merit, the debate rages on, and at great financial waste to us, the taxpayers who foot the bill for this continuing nonsense.

Those who choose to ignore the truth, or rewrite our history for their own prejudicial agendas and those who choose to believe them, need only to refer to the U.S. National Archives on our "Founding Fathers", as reported on the UnderGodProCon.org website;

"Religiously, the men mirrored the overwhelmingly Protestant character of American religious life at the time and were members of various denominations."

The Founding Fathers motivation and inspiration for our nation's founding documents were actually a refined version of the moral, spiritual code of the Holy Bible; the Jewish Torah (the books of Moses, Biblical Old Testament), the Prophets (Old and New Testament), and the "good news" Gospels (New Testament); containing laws against stealing, murder, incest, sexual perversion, etc., are based on God's laws as covenant between Him and his people, whose prosperity depended upon their obedience to the written Law of God (Stone, 2005, pg.18). Perhaps scoffers may be persuaded by a brief review of the Bill of Rights (our God-given rights), which are the first ten amendments to our U.S. Constitution, as listed below:

BILL OF RIGHTS

"1. **Freedom of religion, freedom of speech, freedom of the press, and freedom of assembly and petition;** 2. **The right to bear arms;** 3. **Limit's the quartering of soldiers;** 4. **Limits searches and seizures;** 5. **The right to due process of law, including protection against self-incrimination;** 6. **Rights of a person accused of a crime, including the right to be represented by a lawyer;** 7. **Jury trial in civil cases;** 8. **Unfair bail, fines, and punishment forbidden;** 9. **Citizens entitled to rights not listed in the Constitution;** 10. **Powers reserved to the states or the people.**"

The first amendment, **"Freedom of religion, speech, press, assembly and petition"**, YOUR God-given freedoms are currently in jeopardy, and could potentially be forever corrupted, by the passing of a bill called the "fairness doctrine". This basically says you are no longer free to verbally express your own opinion, or religious doctrines, unless you give equal time to all opposing views, whether transmitted via television, or preached from a church, synagogue, or mosque, and could very well do away with our first Constitutional amendment altogether, and with it, our God-given speech freedoms and entitlements.

If this is passed into law, many well-intended potentially safety-issues could become warped or twisted into "hate-speech" or worse yet, "hate-crimes". We would not even be able to speak out against terrorist organizations who have the explicit intentions of destroying life and liberty (yours and mine, and theirs), without having to spit out a little equal-time to "terrorism-sensitivity-and-culturally-enlightened-awareness" dribblings, or possibly do jail time. And don't dare speak out against child pornography issues, because there is nothing "fair", decent or moral about this, to give potentially mandated "equal time" to.

The new "fairness doctrine" legislation, if passed, would be 100 percent unconstitutional and could very well be subtitled the "oxymoron clause". Freedom of religion would be sanctioned, freedom of speech would be silenced, freedom of the press, assembly and petition would mean being monitored and watched, vis-a-vis, NO MORE FREEDOM.

Our United States Constitution, with all its articles and amendments, is prefaced by the "Preamble" which clearly defines the very essence of, and purpose for the Constitution, and could very well have been the Founding Father's "Mission Statement" for our new fledgling nation.

THE PREAMBLE TO THE U.S. CONSTITUTION

"We the people of the United States,
in order to form a more perfect Union,
establish Justice, insure domestic Tranquility,
provide for the common defence,
promote the general Welfare,
and secure the Blessings of Liberty
to ourselves and our Posterity,
do ordain and establish this Constitution
for the United States of America."

CHAPTER 7

SEPARATION OF CHURCH & STATE

According to all the documentation I found on the religious beliefs of our Founding Fathers, it appears that they ALL believed in God and the Judeo-Christian doctrines they wrote into the founding documents. And other than a few more recent books written on our nation's founding, with references to Christianity inexcusably deleted, or gratuitously mentioned as a mere afterthought or brief human-weakness anecdote, as in the children's book Scholastic Encyclopedia of Presidents and Their Times, by David Rubel, (updated?) 2005; or the disappointing American Creation, "Triumphs and Tragedies at the Founding of the Republic", by Joseph Ellis (Pulitzer Prize winning author), 2007. James Dobson of "Focus on the Family", claims (as do many others) that there are too many authors and judges rewriting our history and our Constitution.

There is nothing at all in our Constitution stating *"a wall of separation between church and state"*, nor any other founding documents. Thomas Jefferson was credited with this statement, from a personal letter to the Danbury Baptists, in response to a letter he had received from them. Please read both letters, and you decide for yourself if Mr. Jefferson intended his words to be used on any founding document, or any form of legislature, as our 20th Century High Court purposely chose to misinterpret for the sake of rewriting our Constitution. The letter from the Danbury Baptist Association, the state of Connecticut, assembled October 7, 1801, (as copied directly from Wallbuilders resources online).

To Thomas Jefferson, Esq., President of the United States of America
Sir,
Among the many millions in America and Europe who rejoice in your election to office, we embrace the first opportunity which we have enjoyed in our collective capacity, since your inauguration, to express our great satisfaction in your appointment to the Chief Magistracy in the United States. And though the mode of expression may be less courtly and pompous than what many others clothe their addresses with, we beg you, sir, to believe, that none is more sincere.

Our sentiments are uniformly on the side of religious liberty: that Religion is at all times and places a matter between God and individuals, that no man ought to suffer in name, person, or effects on account of his religious opinions, (and) that the legitimate power of civil government extends no further than to punish the man who works ill to his neighbor. But sir, our constitution of government is not specific. Our ancient charter, together with the laws made coincident therewith, were adapted as the basis of our government at the time of our revolution. And such has been our laws and usages, and such still are, (so) that Religion is considered as the first object of Legislation, and therefore what religious privileges we enjoy (as a minor part of the State) we enjoy as favors granted, and not as inalienable rights. And these favors we receive at the expense of such degrading acknowledgments, as are inconsistent with the rights of freemen. It is not to be wondered at therefore, if those who seek after power and gain, under the pretense of government and Religion, should reproach their fellow men, (or) should reproach their Chief Magistrate, as an enemy of religion, law, and good order, because he will not, dares not, assume the prerogative of Jehovah and make laws to govern the Kingdom of Christ.

Sir, we are sensible that the President of the United States is not the National legislator and also sensible that the national government cannot destroy the laws of each State, but our hopes are strong that the sentiment of our beloved President, which have had such genial effect already, like the radiant beams of the sun, will shine and prevail through all these States--and all the world--until hierarchy and tyranny be destroyed from the earth. Sir, when we reflect on your past services, and see a glow of philanthropy and goodwill shining forth in a course of more than thirty years, we have reason to believe that America's God has raised you up to fill the Chair of State out of that goodwill which he bears to the millions which you preside over. May God strengthen you for the arduous task which providence and the voice of the people have called you--to sustain and support you and your Administration against all the predetermined opposition of those who wish to rise to wealth and importance on the poverty and subjection of the people.

And may the Lord preserve you safe from every evil and bring you at last to his Heavenly Kingdom through Jesus Christ our Glorious Mediator.
Signed in behalf of the Association,
The Committee

President Jefferson's reply with applicable phrases in parenthesis and/or underlined:

*To the Committee of the Danbury Baptist Association, in the State of Connecticut
Washington, January 1, 1802*

Gentlemen,
The affectionate sentiment of esteem and approbation which you are so good as to express towards me, on behalf of the Danbury Baptist Association, give me the highest satisfaction. My duties dictate a faithful and zealous pursuit of the interests of my constituents, and in proportion as they are persuaded of my fidelity to those duties, the discharge of them becomes more and more pleasing.

Believing with you that religion is a matter which lies solely between man and his God, that He owes account to none other for his faith or his worship, that the legislative powers of government reach actions only, and not opinions, I contemplate with sovereign reverence that act of the whole American people which declared that their legislature would "make no law respecting an establishment of religion, or prohibiting the free exercise thereof," <u>thus building a wall of separation between Church and State.</u> Adhering to this expression of the supreme will of the nation in behalf of the rights of conscience, I shall see with sincere satisfaction the progress of those sentiments which tend to restore to man all his natural rights convinced he has no natural right in opposition to his social duties.

I reciprocate your kind prayers for the protection and blessing of the common Father and Creator of man, and tender you for yourselves and your religious association, assurances of my high respect and esteem.

Th. Jefferson
Jan. 1, 1802

How do you interpret, or better yet, what is your understanding of Jefferson's words?

My understanding certainly was different from the Supreme Court Judge who arbitrarily injected this phrase into OUR Constitution, into OUR country's founding documents!

Who gave him the right to misinterpret this private letter for his own agenda? Why are we allowing this to happen to us? These megalomaniac judges are NOT doing this for our good, but their own personal promotion and to avoid dealing with issues that must be voted upon, with the majority rule. They work for us, we pay their salaries, why aren't we taking a stand and doing something to admonish them for their bad behavior?

Many other websites, television programs and the <u>actual founding documents</u> concur, such as ACHW.org, yet unfortunately many college-level government course texts (which I took, mandatory for lower-level graduation) and other websites which unquestioningly (without researching the facts) accept Supreme Court Justice Black's purposeful misinterpretation of Jefferson's words as well as the fictional "establishment" clause (and that ever-popular "establishment" clause test!?), as though they were written right in the Constitution, and are NOT! I know the original calligraphy handwriting is a bit difficult to read, however our Constitution is available for everyone to see and read, and I strongly recommend reading the original!

This has become the current trend amongst our Judges (unable to read or research the truth without changing it?), who were not appointed to their post, nor elected to their offices to, either accidentally or arbitrarily, "re-do" what our Founding Fathers already did so perfectly under Divine guidance and blessings, based upon devout religious beliefs! And should you agree with the "new-age" (non-researching) authors of today, who absurdly contend that our Founding Fathers were all atheist, please read the following direct quotes of our Declaration and Constitutional framers and signers.

Charters of Freedom

Declaration of Independence

The Constitution

The unanimous Declaration of the thirteen united States of America

When in the Course of human events, it becomes necessary for one people to dissolve the political bands which have connected them with another, and to assume among the powers of the earth, the separate and equal station to which the Laws of Nature and of Nature's God entitle them, a decent respect to the opinions of mankind requires that they should declare the causes which impel them to the separation.

We hold these truths to be self-evident, that all men are created equal, that they are endowed by their Creator with certain unalienable Rights, that among these are Life, Liberty and the pursuit of Happiness. That to secure these rights, Governments are instituted among Men, deriving their just powers from the consent of the governed. That whenever any Form of Government becomes destructive of these ends, it is the Right of the People to alter or to abolish it, and to institute new Government, laying its foundation on such principles and organizing its powers in such form, as to them shall seem most likely to effect their Safety and Happiness. Prudence, indeed, will dictate that Governments long established should not be changed for light and transient causes; and accordingly all experience hath shewn, that mankind are more disposed to suffer, while evils are sufferable, than to right themselves by abolishing the forms to which they are accustomed. But when a long train of abuses and usurpations, pursuing invariably the same Object evinces a design to reduce them under absolute Despotism, it is their right, it is their duty, to throw off such Government, and to provide new Guards for their future security.—Such has been the patient sufferance of these Colonies; and such is now the necessity which constrains them to alter their former Systems of Government. The history of the present King of Great Britain is a history of repeated injuries and usurpations, all having in direct object the establishment of an absolute Tyranny over these States. To prove this, let Facts be submitted to a candid world.

He has refused his Assent to Laws, the most wholesome and necessary for the public good.

He has forbidden his Governors to pass Laws of immediate and pressing importance, unless suspended in their operation till his Assent should be obtained; and when so suspended, he has utterly neglected to attend to them.

He has refused to pass other Laws for the accommodation of large districts of people, unless those people would relinquish the right of Representation in the Legislature, a right inestimable to them and formidable to tyrants only.

He has called together legislative bodies at places unusual, uncomfortable, and distant from the depository of their public Records, for the sole purpose of fatiguing them into compliance with his measures.

He has dissolved Representative Houses repeatedly, for opposing with manly firmness his invasions on the rights of the people.

He has refused for a long time, after such dissolutions, to cause others to be elected; whereby the Legislative powers, incapable of Annihilation, have returned to the People at large for their exercise; the State remaining in the mean time exposed to all the dangers of invasion from without, and convulsions within.

He has endeavoured to prevent the population of these States; for that purpose obstructing the Laws for Naturalization of Foreigners; refusing to pass others to encourage their migrations hither, and raising the conditions of new Appropriations of Lands.

He has obstructed the Administration of Justice, by refusing his Assent to Laws for establishing Judiciary powers.

He has made Judges dependent on his Will alone, for the tenure of their offices, and the amount and payment of their salaries.

He has erected a multitude of New Offices, and sent hither swarms of Officers to harrass our people, and eat out their substance.

He has kept among us, in times of peace, Standing Armies without the Consent of our legislatures.

He has affected to render the Military independent of and superior to the Civil power.

He has combined with others to subject us to a jurisdiction foreign to our constitution, and unacknowledged by our laws; giving his Assent to their Acts of pretended Legislation:

For Quartering large bodies of armed troops among us:

For protecting them, by a mock Trial, from punishment for any Murders which they should commit on the Inhabitants of these States:

For cutting off our Trade with all parts of the world:

For imposing Taxes on us without our Consent:

For depriving us in many cases, of the benefits of Trial by Jury:

For transporting us beyond Seas to be tried for pretended offences:

For abolishing the free System of English Laws in a neighbouring Province, establishing therein an Arbitrary government, and enlarging its Boundaries so as to render it at once an example and fit instrument for introducing the same absolute rule into these Colonies:

For taking away our Charters, abolishing our most valuable Laws, and altering fundamentally the Forms of our Governments:

For suspending our own Legislatures, and declaring themselves invested with power to legislate for us in all cases whatsoever.

He has abdicated Government here, by declaring us out of his Protection and waging War against us.

He has plundered our seas, ravaged our Coasts, burnt our towns, and destroyed the lives of our people.

He is at this time transporting large Armies of foreign Mercenaries to compleat the works of death, desolation and tyranny, already begun with circumstances of Cruelty & perfidy scarcely paralleled in the most barbarous ages, and totally unworthy the Head of a civilized nation.

He has constrained our fellow Citizens taken Captive on the high Seas to bear Arms against their Country, to become the executioners of their friends and Brethren, or to fall themselves by their Hands.

He has excited domestic insurrections amongst us, and has endeavoured to bring on the inhabitants of our frontiers, the merciless Indian Savages, whose known rule of warfare, is an undistinguished destruction of all ages, sexes and conditions.

In every stage of these Oppressions We have Petitioned for Redress in the most humble terms: Our repeated Petitions have been answered only by repeated injury. A Prince whose character is thus marked by every act which may define a Tyrant, is unfit to be the ruler of a free people.

Nor have We been wanting in attentions to our British brethren. We have warned them from time to time of attempts by their legislature to extend an unwarrantable jurisdiction over us. We have reminded them of the circumstances of our emigration and settlement here. We have appealed to their native justice and magnanimity, and we have conjured them by the ties of our common kindred to disavow these usurpations, which, would inevitably interrupt our connections and correspondence. They too have been deaf to the voice of justice and of consanguinity. We must, therefore, acquiesce in the necessity, which denounces our Separation, and hold them, as we hold the rest of mankind, Enemies in War, in Peace Friends.

We, therefore, the Representatives of the united States of America, in General Congress, Assembled, appealing to the Supreme Judge of the world for the rectitude of our intentions, do, in the Name, and by Authority of the good People of these Colonies, solemnly publish and declare, That these United Colonies are, and of Right ought to be Free and Independent States; that they are Absolved from all Allegiance to the British Crown, and that all political connection between them and the State of Great Britain, is and ought to be totally dissolved; and that as Free and Independent States, they have full Power to levy War, conclude Peace, contract Alliances, establish Commerce, and to do all other Acts and Things which Independent States may of right do. And for the support of this Declaration, with a firm reliance on the protection of divine Providence, we mutually pledge to each other our Lives, our Fortunes and our sacred Honor.

Quotes from our Founding Fathers regarding their devout religious beliefs, courtesy of Center For Moral Clarity.net website.

George Washington: *"I have often expressed my sentiments, that every man, conducting himself as a good citizen, and being accountable to God alone for his religious opinions, ought to be protected in worshipping the Deity according to the dictates of his own conscience."*

"No people can be bound to acknowledge and adore the invisible hand, which conducts the Affairs of men more than the People of the United States. Every step, by which they have advanced to the character of an independent nation, seems to have been distinguished by some token of providential agency."

James Madison: *"It is impossible for the man of pious reflection not to perceive in it (the Constitution) a finger of the Almighty hand which has been so frequently and signally extended to our relief in the critical stages of the revolution."*

"It is the duty of every man to render to the Creator such homage and such only as he believes to be acceptable to him. This duty is precedent, both in order of time and in degree of obligation, to the claims of Civil Society."

"We have staked the whole future of American civilization, not upon the power of government, far from it. We have staked the future . . . Upon the capacity of each and all of us to govern ourselves, to sustain ourselves, according to the Ten Commandments of God."

John Adams: *"It is the duty of all men in society, publicly, and at stated seasons, to worship the SUPREME BEING, the great Creator, and Preserver of the universe. And no subject shall be hurt, molested, or restrained, in his person, liberty, or estate, for worshipping GOD in the manner most agreeable to the dictates of his own conscience; or for his religious profession or sentiments, provided he doth not disturb the public peace, or obstruct others in their religious worship."*

"The moment the idea is admitted into society that property is not as sacred as the laws of God, and that there is not a force of law and public justice to protect it, anarchy and tyranny commence. If 'Thou shalt not covet' and 'Thou shalt not steal' were not commandments of Heaven, they must be made inviolable precepts in every society before it can be civilized or made free."

Thomas Paine: *"But where says some is the King of America? I'll tell you Friend, He Reigns above, and doth not make havoc of mankind like the Royal brute of Britain . . . Let it be brought forth placed on the Divine law, the word of God; let a crown be placed thereon, by which the world may know, that so far as we approve of monarchy, that in America THE LAW IS KING."*

"I believe in one God, and no more; and I hope for happiness beyond this life. I believe in the equality of humans; and I believe that religious duties consist in doing justice, loving mercy, and endeavoring to make our fellow creatures happy."

Benjamin Franklin: *"All of us who were engaged in the struggle must have observed frequent instances of Superintending Providence in our favor. To that kind Providence we owe this happy opportunity of consulting in peace on the means of establishing our future national felicity. And have we now forgotten that powerful friend? Or do we imagine that we no longer need His assistance? I have lived, Sir, a long time, and the longer I live, the more convincing proofs I see of this truth-that God governs in the affairs of men. And if a sparrow cannot fall to the ground without His Notice, is it probable that and Empire can rise without his Aid?"*

"That wise Men have in all Ages thought Government necessary for the Good of Mankind; and that wise Governments have always thought Religion necessary for the well ordering and well-being of Society."

Alexander Hamilton: *"To grant that there is a Supreme Intelligence who rules the world and has established laws to regulate the actions of his creatures; and still to assert that man, in a state of nature, may be considered as perfectly free from all restraints of law and government, appears to a common understanding altogether irreconcilable. Good and wise men, in all ages, have embraced a very dissimilar theory. They have supposed that the deity, from the relations we stand in to himself and to each other, has constituted an eternal and immutable law, which is indispensably obligatory upon all mankind, prior to any human* *institution whatever. This is what is called the law of nature . . . Upon this law depend the natural rights of mankind."*

". . . natural liberty is a gift of the beneficent Creator to the whole human race, and that civil liberty is founded in that; and cannot be wrested from any people, without the most manifest violation of justice."

Thomas Jefferson: *"And can the liberties of a nation be thought secure when we have removed their only firm basis, a conviction in the minds of the people that these liberties are the gift of God? That they are not to be violated but with His wrath? Indeed I tremble for my country when I reflect that God is just: that His justice cannot sleep forever."*

"In matters of religion, I have considered that its free exercise is placed by the Constitution independent of the powers of the General (federal) Government."

The Cape Henry Landing by Stephen Reid

From these very shores the Gospel shall go forth to not only this New World, but the entire world.

Reverend Robert Hunt
April 29, 1607

Our Spiritual Heritage

First Landing

The movie every American needs to see.

CHAPTER 8

COLONIZATION OF AMERICA

We all learned the Christopher Columbus story in grade school, by learning the rhyme;

"In fourteen hundred and ninety-two, Columbus sailed the ocean blue . . ."

continuing with the names of his three ships, *"the Nina, the Pinta and Santa Maria."* Sponsored by the King and Queen of Spain, looking for the Orient, to trade for spices, Christopher Columbus bumped into the West Indies, where he planted a cross, eventually happened onto the Americas, by mistake, and assuming he had found India, named the "locals" Indians. After several long trips between Europe and America (which he believed was his Divine calling), he died in 1506, still looking for a short-cut to the Orient through Central America, at Panama.

One hundred years later, in 1607, the first English settlers led by Captain John Smith led 144 men, three ships, and a commissioned Chaplain, Vicar Robert Hunt, across the Atlantic Ocean to the New World. The "first landing" was at Cape Henry Beach, Virginia, which would later become First Landing State Park, where these explorers and missionaries planted a seven-foot-tall cross in the sand, dedicating the New World to Jesus Christ, claiming it for the glory of God. While the first permanent English settlement was being founded in Jamestown, Virginia, Reverend Hunt established the first Protestant Church there in America.

Reclaiming the Covenant

From these very shores the Gospel shall go forth to not only this New World, but the entire world.

This was the prayer of Reverend Robert Hunt on April 29, 1607,
as he dedicated America to our Lord Jesus Christ for His glory and purpose.

In remembrance of the 400th anniversary of that sacred moment in time,
The Christian Broadcasting Network is privileged to recognize

Cheri Majors

for reclaiming the holy covenant of 1607 by reaffirming that America is dedicated
to our Lord Jesus Christ, for His glory and purpose, and confirming our nation's mission as described in the
prayer of our forefather: ... *the Gospel shall go forth to not only this New World, but the entire world.*

Pat Robertson
CBN Founder and Chairman

In 1620, the Pilgrims (many later calling themselves Puritans), also of a deep Christian faith, came to Plymouth Rock, Cape Cod, Massachusetts, and lost half their numbers in the first harsh New England winter. However, with the help of an Indian, taken away by "slavers" and raised in Europe, they learned how to survive in the new land. They celebrated their first harvest which became our first Thanksgiving, giving thanks to God (not corn-husk spirits, or rock carvings).

By 1629, the Massachusetts Bay Colony was founded and Congregationalism was established in the New World. In 1634, the Roman Catholic Church was established and the state of Maryland was founded. In 1636, Rhode Island was founded as a safe-haven for religious dissidents not agreeing with the strict Puritan ways. In 1654, Jewish refugees arrive in New York, and build synagogues, after fleeing Brazil from religious persecution. And in 1682, the Quakers founded the state of Pennsylvania.

Religious denominations were inching West while spreading South, populating Georgia and the Carolinas. Many early American colonies were settled by groups seeking religious freedom but who were themselves intolerant of religious dissent (Cummings & Wise, 2001, pg. 99).

The remnants of a strong Roman Catholic presence in Louisiana's beginnings, lingers today as their counties are divided into "Parishes". The Spanish Catholic influence is prevalent throughout the Southwest but especially in California, as our state's religious heritage is documented through the "mission trail" up and down our California coastline.

In an effort to populate California, Spain authorized a coastal chain of missions to be built up the coastline in 1767. These missions were to be about a days horseback ride apart and the road connecting them became known as El Camino Real (the Royal or King's Road, in Spanish). The first missions were established by Catholic Father Junipero Serra and were the major focal point of every community the missions were built in.

The missions served as church, school, farm, and hospital, employing as well as caring for its members. The coastal communities we have today were started by the missions, as the emerging towns grew out of them, or directly around them. The missions and Padres (Fathers, or Priests in Spanish), provided everything the people needed, spreading Christianity and God's word at Mass (church services) in the chapel, educating the children in mission classrooms using the Bible as the textbook, healing the sick, and employing the community on massive mission farms. This was the beginning of California's Christian heritage, which supplied all other needs, from education, nutrition, irrigation, agricultural, hospital care, employment, and our "community" heritage.

At the same time California was being tamed and colonized out West, the East Coast was founding our nation's first schools and Universities, which were established as public seminaries, to train ministers and missionaries to go out into the world to spread the Gospel of Jesus Christ. Their only textbook was the Holy Bible at those distinguished Universities which helped shape our nation, and they're still standing today. Those schools are Harvard, Yale, and Princeton Universities.

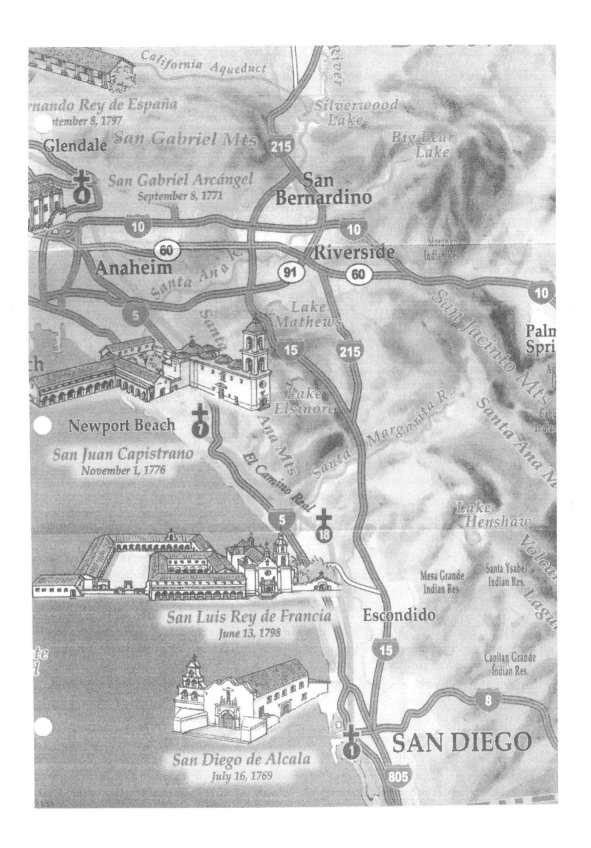

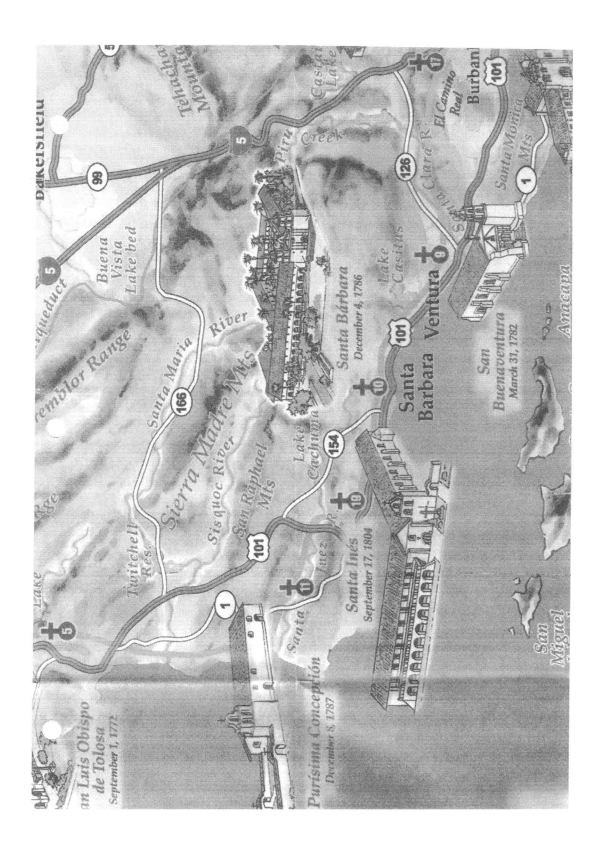

PART III

WORLD VIEWS

&

PRACTICES

"To the pure all things are pure, but to those who are defiled and unbelieving nothing is pure; but even their mind and conscious are defiled. They profess to know God, but in works they deny Him, being abominable, disobedient, and disqualified for every good work."

Titus 1:15-16

Holidays Around the World

By Robin Griggs Lawrence

Italy
La Vigilia (Feast of the Seven Fishes) December 24

Following a tradition that began in Sicily, many Italians (and Italian-Americans) share a completely fish-based Christmas Eve meal known as La Vigilia or the Feast of the Seven Fishes. Many believe serving seven fish dishes honors the Catholic Church's seven sacraments, although interpretations of the number's symbolism vary. In any case, this delicious tradition is tied to the Catholic practice of eating no meat for 24 hours before Christmas Day. The excitement of waiting for Christmas Day, when Catholics celebrate the birth of their Savior, reaches its peak as Italians feast on antipasto, pasta, and main dishes made with salted cod, eel, calamari, smelts, tuna, crab, clams, and anchovies. Savoy cabbage and stuffed peppers are traditional side dishes.

Mexico
Las Posadas (December 16–24), Día de los Reyes (January 6), La Fiesta del Monito (February 2)

Las Posadas (which means "inn" or "shelter") launches Mexico's holiday season with nine days of candlelight processions. Every afternoon groups of "Holy Pilgrims" re-enact Mary and Joseph's search for an inn through a procession headed by a young girl representing the Virgen Maria. She's followed by children dressed in silver and gold robes carrying walking staffs, paper lanterns, or candles. The procession visits two houses and is told there's no room at the inn. At the third house, everyone is invited in for a party featuring Christmas carols, piñatas and hot chocolate.

At Día de los Reyes (Feast of the Epiphany), Mexicans celebrate the Three Wise Men's journey following the star of Bethlehem to baby Jesus. Children leave their shoes outside filled with hay; the Wise Men come by to feed their horses and leave gifts in exchange. The highlight of the Epiphany feast is the king's crown cake, rosca de reyes (available in the U.S. at most bakeries), a crown-shaped glazed bread made with walnuts, grated orange peel, raisins, and candied cherries with a small figure of a baby and a coin baked inside. The person who gets the coin has good luck for the new year. Whoever gets the baby is the king or queen of the celebration but also has to give another party on or before Candlemas (La Fiesta del Monito), which heralds the presentation of baby Jesus in the Temple, and marks the official end of Mexico's holiday season.

Islam
Ramadan October 4–November 2

Ramadan is held during the ninth month of the Muslim calendar, when Allah revealed the first verses of the Koran, the holy book of Islam, to the prophet Muhammad. It's a time of intense worship, charity, purifying behavior, and good deeds. To commemorate the month, more than a billion Muslims worldwide fast during daylight hours and focus on worship, contemplation, and strengthening family and community ties. Fasting reminds Muslims of how the poor suffer, teaches them appreciation, and cleanses both their bodies and their minds. Each day they break the fast by sharing an evening meal that begins with dates and sweet drinks for a quick energy boost. Ramadan ends with the festival of Eid al-Fitr (Festival of Breaking the Fast), where people dress in their finest clothes, decorate their homes, and give treats to children.

Sweden
Santa Lucia (Festival of Lights) December 13

The Festival of Lights celebrates Lucia, a martyred Roman saint known for her kindness and love, whose name means "light" (from the Latin *lux*). Mothers in Sweden wake their children before dawn to prepare Lussekatter (X-shaped buns) to quell hunger and candles to light the darkness. The family eats breakfast by candlelight. Later, girls wear white dresses with crimson sashes and crowns made from greenery and seven (now battery-powered) candles, while boys wear white pointy hats with gold stars for Santa Lucia processions. The children bring Lucíapepparkakor (spicy gingerbread biscuits), Julglogg (mulled wine), and coffee to homes, hospitals, factories, and offices.

India
Diwali (Festival of Lights) November 1–5

The most important and exciting festival in India, Diwali is a five-day new year's celebration that focuses on family gatherings, feasting, and giving gifts. Diwali means rows of lighted lamps. The holiday is named after the diyas (oil lamps in earthen containers) placed in rows around homes and commercial buildings to greet Laksmi, the goddess of wealth. The lamps also symbolize knowledge and remind people to reflect on the celebration's true meaning. Fireworks are exploded, and doorways are decorated with torans of mango leaves and marigolds or with rangolis, intricate designs made with rangoli powder. Sweets and dried fruits, as well as expensive gifts such as jewelry, are exchanged, and women often buy gold, silver, or new utensils.

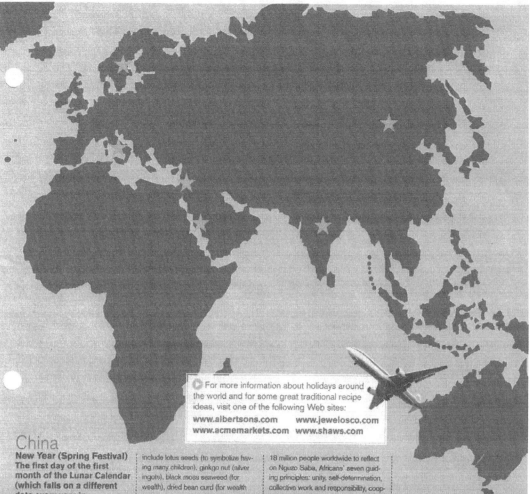

> For more information about holidays around the world and for some great traditional recipe ideas, visit one of the following Web sites:
> www.albertsons.com www.jewelosco.com
> www.acmemarkets.com www.shaws.com

China
New Year (Spring Festival)
The first day of the first month of the Lunar Calendar (which falls on a different date every year in January or February of the Western calendar). For 2006, Chinese New Year falls on January 26.

New Year, China's most important holiday, starts on the first day of the New Year and ends with the Yuen Xiao Festival (Lantern Festival) on the fifteenth day of the month. Families gather on New Year's Eve for a family dinner known as *Tuan Nien*, or "family reunion." Even departed family members travel back home for the feast. It is an important occasion for the families. Huge feasts are prepared to bring abundance. These usually include a dish of "jai" (with different kinds of vegetables or produce). The jai dish may include lotus seeds (to symbolize having many children), ginkgo nut (silver ingots), black moss seaweed (for wealth), dried bean curd (for wealth and happiness), and bamboo shoots (for all to be well). Other dishes include a whole fish (which represents in abundance, with surplus), a whole chicken with its head, tail, and feet to symbolize completeness (for prosperity), and uncut noodles (to symbolize long life). At midnight, firecrackers are lit to drive away evil spirits.

African-American
Kwanzaa
December 26–January 1

With its focus on family, community, and self-improvement, Kwanzaa is a time for African-Americans to reaffirm their African culture. Founded in 1966, Kwanzaa is an occasion for more than 18 million people worldwide to reflect on Nguzo Saba, Africans' seven guiding principles: unity, self-determination, collective work and responsibility, cooperative economics, purpose, creativity, and faith. The word *kwanzaa* comes from the Kiswahili phrase matunda ya kwanza, "first fruits of the harvest." The holiday is rooted in African harvest celebrations and includes a communal feast on December 31. Homes are decorated in black, red, and green with a traditional Kwanzaa setting: a candleholder with seven candles (one black, three red, three green), a basket of vegetables, a straw placemat, a unity cup, and an ear of corn for every child.

Judaism
Hanukkah (Festival of Lights)
December 25–January 1

Hanukkah is an eight-day celebration commemorating the Maccabees' victory over the Syrian army. When the Jews rededicated the Temple of Solomon in Jerusalem, they found only one day's worth of oil to light the holy lamps of the menorah, but all the lamps stayed lit for eight days. On the first night of Hanukkah, Jews say blessings and light two candles (one known as the *shamash* or "servant" candle to light the others) on a candelabra called a *menorah*. Each night another candle is lit until all eight are aglow. During Hanukkah celebrations children receive *gelt* (chocolate coins wrapped in gold foil) and small gifts and play with a *dreidel*, a four-sided spinning top. Many Hanukkah dishes, including *latkes* (potato pancakes) and *sufganiot* (jelly doughnuts), are fried to symbolize the oil that burned for eight days.

Robin Griggs Lawrence spent last Christmas with her two children in France.

CHAPTER 9

HOLIDAYS

Just as our first and highly prestigious Universities of Harvard, Princeton, and Yale were created for Judeo-Christian theological studies, as was the fabric of our nation's founding, so too, were other schools started for younger students, teaching them to read by use of the scriptures in their textbook, the Bible. Since then (not even 250 years later), a dried-up or "neutered" higher-learning academia has overtaken our classrooms at every grade level, from preschool to college. That neutering process has stripped away our passion for learning without the accountability to God, our nation, our families, and each other. We have allowed our religious "backbone" heritage, and all thematically corresponding traditions and festive Christian holidays to be removed, one-by-one, against our will.

A Gallup poll of just over a thousand adults in early Spring, 2005, showed that 84 percent of them identified with a Christian religion (and celebrate the Christmas holiday). I also know many families of different faiths residing in Southern California who openly celebrate Christmas right along with us. However, all we hold dear is being castrated from our educational institutions and our religious founding history, ripping out Christianity by the roots. What happened to our national Christmas holiday, Good Friday, and Easter (I am aware the term Easter is pagan) but should we call it, the Jesus died-on-the-cross-for-our-sins "Crucifixion", "Resurrection" rose-from-the-dead-after-3-days, for our "Eternal

Salvation" so-we-can-have-a-better-life holiday week? Our School Board Administrators and Legislators have renamed our Christian holidays for us (out of respect, for whom?) from Easter to "Spring Break", Good Friday is non-existent, and Christmas has now forfeited to the "Winter Break", decorated by meaningless snowmen and dancing reindeer.

The ACLU (American Civil Liberties Union) has surgically suited up, slumming through the nation's highways and byways, desperately scourging for any mention of "Christ", whether Christmas, the word or holiday, nativity scenes, school pageants, caroling, or symbols such as crucifixes or crosses (as discussed in earlier chapters, with a huge price tag for the taxpayers, who have to foot-the-bill for revised letterhead, business cards, pamphlets, checks, etc., re-printed, and re-distributed to the tune of hundreds of thousands of dollars - OUR dollars, and by-the-way superfluous legal action is just as costly to all of us!

I would hope the ACLU would pitch-in some of their excess cash or time toward more economic stimulus checks to help re-start our dying economy. They just plug along excessively suing and threatening law suits, taking our court time, our tax dollars, and our Christian (America's documented founding faith doctrine) dignity, right along with our promised blessings. How long are we going to allow this to continue? And should the "fairness doctrine" pass legislature, it could mean equal-time for faith-based holiday celebrations. Meaning life as we know it now could become quite a circus; *"Lions and tigers and bears, oh my!"*

Claremont Human Services

SPECIAL EVENTS

CITY OF CLAREMONT
Calendar of E·V·E·N·T·S

Celebrate Claremont!

You are invited to share in Claremont's community spirit. A variety of free and low-cost family events are held throughout the year. For more information on any of these events, please call the City of Claremont Human Services Dept. at (909) 399-5490.

Walking Tour Depot Downtown	1st Saturday of Each Month *10 am - 11:45 am*
Cruise Night	2nd Saturday of Each Month *March - October*
 Spring Egg Hunt	Saturday, March 26 *9-11 am, Memorial Park*
Western Round-Up *Our Lady of the Assumption Church*	May 6-8 *Contact: Jean McKenna, 626-3596*
City Wide Yard Sale	Saturday-May 7 *9 am-Noon, Cahuilla Park*
Independence Day Celebration	Monday-July 4 *Memorial Park - Pomona College*
Children's Concert Series	Wednesdays, July 6-27 *7-8 pm, Memorial Park*
Monday Night Concert Series	Mondays, July 11- Sept 5 *7:30-9 pm, Memorial Park*
Movies in the Park	Fridays, Aug 5 & 12 *Dusk, Larkin Park*
Depot Jazz Series	Fridays, Sept 16-Oct 14 *Village Depot Station*
Village Venture	Saturday, October 22 *9 am-5 pm, Claremont Village*
Halloween Carnival	Monday, October 31 *5:30-8 pm, Cahuilla Park*
Veterans Day	Friday, November 11

If your organization would like to be a part of providing quality of life programs in our community, contact Ali Martinez, Special Events Coordinator Human Services (909) 399-5491

I don't know how you feel about this new doctrine of "fairness" (we, as Christians have always tried to be fair), but I don't really want to celebrate my glorious Christmases while having to give equal-time to "Allah" by fasting for a "Ramadan" journey with their "Mohammad", or being forced to light candles throughout my house or church for the Hindu "Diwali" (as beautiful as that seems, it's a fire hazard).

The only reason there are so many other faiths in our country is because Christianity is the "open arms" faith, accepting and allowing all faiths to take refuge here, as we did. Yet we are crumbling as a nation without God and our Judeo-Christian faith at the fore-front. We are still fumbling to pick up our brokenness from 911 (attack against our country that brought down New York's Twin Towers), Hurricane Katrina (decayed levees flooded states above the Gulf of Mexico and along the Mississippi River, while government and response agencies seemingly couldn't do anything to help).

Middle Easterners call us "Infidels" and our flag is burned in European, South American, and African countries (if they're unable to drag our soldiers, beating them to their deaths). And to my horror, I witnessed two men hanging out of their car window cheering (the Middle Eastern tongue warble while waving clinched fists, driving on our streets), the morning of 911, in Southern California, just hours after the New York, Pentagon, and foiled-Washington D.C. attacks. What is going to wake us up to the fact we need to get back to our Christian roots, our God, His word in our Bibles, our holidays and traditions, and our love and concern for one another, because only then will we truly have *"the joy of the Lord in our hearts"*.

News anchor John Gibson takes a political and personal look at how Christmas is under attack by liberals here in America. From court decisions to remove nativity scenes, to ACLU threats over the use of the word "Christmas" in school documents, the holiday celebrating Christ's birth has become a battleground, a war zone where Christian faith is pitted against secular humanism in a fight that often leaves children and morality as unfortunate victims.

PUBLISHER'S EDITION $24.95
➤ MEMBER'S EDITION $15.99
95-9810

NEW! SAVE 36% OFF PUBLISHER'S EDITION PRICE

In December, 2005, on CBN News, a Jewish man and President of an organization named "Jews Against Anti-Christian Defamation", Don Feder, shared with viewers that (in yet another poll) 96 percent of Americans recognized the United States as a Christian nation who celebrate the Christmas Holiday. According to CBN's online, "Religion Roundup", 2005, others in the Jewish community concur, such as human rights activist Michael Horowitz, Rabbi Daniel Lapin, and comedian Jackie Mason, have all defended Christmas as a positive expression of the religious values making America a safe-haven for the Jewish people (paraphrased).

Books are also being written on this topic, and one in particular which tries to show the "rampant" anti-Christianity view is titled, The War On Christmas, "How the Conspiracy to Subvert Our Most Sacred Holiday Is Worse Than You Thought", by John Gibson, a FOX News Anchor. And do you remember the Target Christmas boycott by Christians not too long ago; when Target could have lost mega-millions in "Christmas-related" retail revenue, and chose to wish us a *"Merry Christmas"* after all?

However it does seem the most difficult for our politicians, namely mayors, governors, and our President, who must send neutral Christmas cards to their constituents, as our beloved actor-turned "Governator", Arnold and wife Maria's 2005, Christmas card harmonized with the controversial dilemma facing President Bush that year. The White House "Holiday Tree" once again became a "Christmas Tree" in 2005, as reported on the PBS news program "Religion & Ethics".

CHAPTER 10

FAITHS

The five main faiths covering the world today, which are represented throughout the United States are: Christianity, Judaism, Islam, Hinduism, and Buddhism. There is, however one new faith trying to take root in our country and the world, a "belief" in nothing, or better known as atheism, which is laying the groundwork for a new "global religion" or "global order".

Europe has been addressing these globally-religious issues with the establishment of the European Union and the "euro" monetary system. Some European countries have opened their borders to neighboring Arabic/Islamic immigrants and refugees, many receiving government subsidies in their new country, however recent rioting over second-class citizenship has been difficult for many to tolerate, therefore, some have since re-closed their borders to them.

Perhaps you heard about the pastor in Sweden who was imprisoned for preaching Biblical precepts against homosexuality, when it was part of his sermon, preached from his own church pulpit. He was charged with a hate-crime. Since when is a Biblical church sermon considered hate-speech? Something similar to the "fairness doctrine" is already in place in the E.U. Now there's talk about an "amero" currency, and a merging of the Americas (North and South), and Canada who's had a "fairness" act or law in place for years now.

The original Constitution was signed in
This was done in 1791. The first 1

1st: Freedom of religion

Symbols of the five major religions

 Christianity

 Judaism

 Islam

 Hinduism

 Buddhism

2nd: Right to bear arms

3rd: Limits the qu soldiers

6th: Rights of a person accused of a crime, including the right to be

An interesting read on the future "global-order" path our schools have been fast-tracking our children down is Brave New Schools, by Berit Kjos, 1995, with charts comparing the practices of ancient pagan faiths to new-age nonsense, and others listing Christian Bible Scripture, to the atheism or humanism statement, to the globalistic or "new-age religious intentions". We have certainly come a long way from our founding Christian roots when we start to view new-age "unity" as an alternative faith, by somehow combining all the conflicting religions to live in peace without setting any boundaries in our nation.

Since the 1600's, America has allowed other faiths to worship and practice according to their beliefs, providing certain laws, God's 10 Commandments handed down by Moses were adhered to. Sanctity-of-life kinds of laws, such as no killing, no stealing, don't sleep around, don't put your vices above God (idol worship), etc., etc. However, we are not always granted the same courtesies in other countries, such as Islamic nations, who won't even let Christian aid/relief workers or Red Cross volunteers help the war-torn or disaster-stricken people without trying to imprison them for erroneous "proselytizing". Or the American news correspondent and others, captured, and beheaded "live" for the web-crowd, and all to see on Al Jezzera T.V. Is this supposed to bolster the terrorist's obvious feelings of "impotent" manhood, or manipulation issues amongst their own people, in-humane scare-tactics, or just blatant ignorance of the "gift of life" promised to all, under Judeo-Christian laws of love?

Televised bayonet-saw-style "beheadings", complete with blood-curdling screams of torture, silenced only by a shredded juggler gushing pulsating lifeblood, and other unspeakable "inhumanities" are allowed in the Muslim faith, according to the Koran or Qur'an (Islam's Holy Book). I quote from Perry Stone's book, <u>Unusual Prophecies Being Fulfilled</u>, "New Insight Into 911", 2005, where he discusses this horrific and psychologically-imbalanced "disorder" passing off as a religion, citing passages from the Qur'an when he says;

> *"Since the beginning of the War on Terror, the entire world has been shocked to see a group of masked Islamic fanatics reading a decree against an innocent man or woman and then literally cutting his head off. The teachings of Mohammad in the Qur'an indicate that beheading is permitted:*
>
>> *'I will cast terror into the hearts of those who disbelieve. Therefore strike off their heads and strike off every fingertip of them. This is because they acted adversely to Allah and His Apostle (8:12, 13).*
>>
>> *Seize them and kill them wherever you find them (4:89).*
>>
>> *When you meet the unbelievers in the battlefield strike off their heads and, when you have laid them low, bind your captives firmly (47:4).'"*

Mr. Stone continues with related Biblical prophesy,

> *"Terrorism on America's shore is a visible warning that our nation has strayed away from God. We have removed prayer and Bible reading from school, legalized abortion and allowed tax money to pay for it, permitted the gay lifestyle to be accepted and promoted, and we are now allowing the removal of Christian symbols and Christian songs from being sung during holiday seasons. Removing these spiritual landmarks is shoving our unbelief in the face of God."*

Do you remember all the rioting and threats made in 2006, because of a cartoon depicting the face of Allah or Mohammad, appearing innocently in a Dutch newspaper? Are Christians the only people-of-faith that others are allowed to poke fun at, legally? It would appear we are confident enough to laugh at ourselves. Christian men just don't have as many "masculine" issues, confidant in their manhood, as appointed by God (and we love them for that). Our women can be bold and funny at the same time, and our children aren't gun-toters (thank God), opting instead for wholesome singing, dancing and Vacation Bible School fun and laughter!

It appears other faiths just don't have as much to laugh about as we do with *"the joy of the Lord in our hearts"*; as their rulers strip them of their freedom, opportunities, even their dignity by denying them food and medicine. I can understand why they would seek

ATTENTION: "LIBERTY 2008" Matching Challenge DOUBLES Your Opportunity to Make a History-Making, Nation-Shaping Impact

American Center for Law & Justice

2008 Freedom Update
A Year Like No Other ... A Pivotal Moment in America's History

Deadline for briefs closing in

Ten Commandments Under Fire

- Two Ten Commandments cases at the Supreme Court: *Summum v. Pleasant Grove City* and *Summum v. Duchesne City*
- Summum organization suing to force display of their "Seven Aphorisms"
- Option: Eliminate display of Ten Commandments
- ACLJ reply briefs due within weeks

Israel under fire

Christians Persecuted, Israel Threatened

- Countering claims of those pushing for peace by dividing the city of Jerusalem
- Move would appease terrorists and put Israel at serious risk
- Also opposing persecution against Christians by Hamas and other terrorist groups
- ACLJ Government Affairs and senior staff teaming with Chief Counsel Jay Alan Sekulow

Abortion Legalized?

- So-called "Freedom of Choice Act" would bar federal government regulation of abortion
- Would defy public polls, act of Congress and President, ruling of Supreme Court
- Passage would mean return of horrific partial-birth abortion practice now outlawed
- ACLJ working hard to see Freedom of Choice Act shelved

Truly serious threat

Pledge of Allegiance Targeted

- Freedom From Religion Foundation, represented by Dr. Michael Newdow, is suing Congress to remove "under God" from Pledge of Allegiance in *Freedom From Religion Foundation v. Congress*
  - Single most serious anti-Pledge lawsuit in history
  - Loss would likely lead to effective ban on God's name in public, including schools

(over)

refuge here, and why they would take themselves and their dire circumstances so seriously (rage and anger issues with feelings of insecurity about their faith, or their "purpose" within it). I too would probably carry a gun around, if forced to live under like circumstances. However, I do not understand at all, why those who relocate here for "better opportunities", can be so vocal and so threatening about stripping us of our faith, faith that made this nation great! Should we start to encourage, legalize, and then enforce sending those "radicals" back home, if it's sooo unbearable for them here in the "land of opportunity".

During a 2005, television interview with Former Secretary of State, John Ashcroft; when asked about world religions, he acknowledged a simple truth (which we should all take time to think about), as he confidently stated,

> *"In other religions you are required to*
> *sacrifice your son for God ----*
>
> *but in Christianity*
>
> *God sacrificed His Son for us!"*

Of all the dispositions and habits which lead to political prosperity, Religion and Morality are indispensable supports. In vain would that man claim the tribute of Patriotism, who should labor to subvert these great pil-

INDISPENSABLE
Supports

lars of human happiness, these firmest props of the duties of Men and Citizens. The mere Politician, equally with the pious man, ought to respect and to cherish them. A volume could not trace all their connections with private and public felicity. Let it simply be asked, Where is the security for property, for reputation, for life, if the sense of religious obligation desert the oaths which are the instruments of investigation in Courts of Justice? And let us with caution indulge the supposition, that morality can be maintained without religion. Whatever may be conceded to the influence of refined education on minds of peculiar structure, reason and experience both forbid us to expect, that national morality can prevail in exclusion of religious principle.

— From the Farewell address of
PRESIDENT GEORGE WASHINGTON,
September 17, 1796

CHAPTER 11

MORALITY

In every "sinking" nation or "decaying" civilization there is a decline in morality, it is the first thing to go, as in ancient Greece. This is a phrase I am hearing repeated over and over again, on different shows, documentaries, and interviews. Taking God and prayer out of schools, out of Christmas, and piece-by-piece removing national monuments, as well as trying to remove Him from our Judeo-Christian founding and trying to delete Him from our history and our daily lives, has removed all societal accountability, boundaries, and sense of morality in our nation.

Other nations see our blatant immorality, internet porn, "adult" movies, over-exposed fashions, drinking, drugs, sexual perversions, and other excesses which have rightly earned us such disreputable names as "infidels", "little Satan", etc. And I could talk more about the detestable abortion "infanticide" issues, as discussed in other chapters, however, the root cause of abortion, is actually the declining "morality" of our nation straying away from its Christian roots, and the blessings thereof.

Founding Father and First President of the United States of America, George Washington, wrote about religion and morality as "indispensable supports" contained within his farewell address, dated September 17, 1796, as copied from "Liberty Magazine" online;

> *"Of all the dispositions and habits, which lead to political prosperity, Religion and Morality are indispensable supports. In vain would that man claim the tribute of Patriotism, who should labor to subvert these great pillars of human happiness, these firmest props of the duties of Men and Citizens. The mere Politician, equally with the pious man, ought to respect and cherish them. A volume could not trace all their connections with private and public felicity. Let it simply be asked,*
>
> > *'Where is the security for property, for reputation, for life, if the sense of religious obligation desert the oaths, which are the instruments of investigation in Courts of Justice?'*
>
> *And let us with caution indulge the supposition, that morality can be maintained without religion. Whatever may be conceded to the influence of refined education or minds of peculiar structure, reason and experience both forbid us to expect, that national morality can prevail in exclusion of religious principle."*

Moral practices do not generally spurn such an onslaught of books, as written within this new Millennium to warn us about the "immoral minority", who have become loud, and obnoxious, a very real threat to our beliefs. Arianna Huffington has written a book titled, <u>Right is Wrong,</u> "How the Lunatic Fringe Hijacked America, Shredded the Constitution, and Made us All Less Safe (and What You Need to Know to End the Madness)" 2007, speaks for itself, and I cannot wait to read it! And many other new books are comparing current events with the last, prophetic Book of the Bible, "Revelation".

A local news program which aired January 1994, following the "Northridge Quake" in Southern California, after a Fall 1993, fire-storm which had consumed much of our area, reported by a visibly-shaken, news anchor, trying to take a lighter approach to what seemed insurmountable destruction, finished his new cast with the question,

"What next? . . . . LOCUSTS?

We all laughed nervously, while asking, where did that come from? Every Christian and Jewish person immediately knew he meant one of God's plagues upon the Egyptians, for not letting His people go, and which are supposed to be repeated in the final days. And there is also an old saying that,

"There are no atheists in foxholes . . .",

Meaning everyone gets religious (possibly smarter) when there's a possibility of death, and you can bet our brave servicemen and women are a religious bunch (America's finest)!.

One of America's finest hours was shortly after 911, when Republicans and Democrats, Senators and Congressmen alike, put their differences aside, stood together on the steps of the Senate Building, and sang "God Bless America". That was enough to bring goose-bumps to my arms, because we were all afraid, yet strong and united in our faith, if even for a moment! The Bible verse that has carried me throughout my life, which truly seems to apply here is:

"I can do all things through Christ,

which strengthens me!"

Philippians 4:13

However, it's a sadly immoral day, when America has trouble passing a "Child Online Protection Act" (COPA), based upon it's supposed unconstitutionality? That our children's rights to protection are not as important as the ACLU and Court of Appeals contends that the online predators and pornography pushers' First Amendment rights would be violated. And worse yet, many predators who have been caught and captured after kidnapping and torturing our children, have only served minimum amounts of jail time and probation.

Another growing concern of mine, and should be to everyone else, is the number of children in foster care, who are taken from loving fost/adopt homes, only to be given back to family members who do not want them, or who have jail records, to repeat the same abuses that Social Services originally removed them from. One case was recently reported on the news, Spring 2008, where a three-year old girl was taken from her fost/adopt home, to live with her biological uncle and aunt who beat her to death, as they had just been released from jail. Shamefully, the judge in that case ruled the fatal beating to be "an accident" because it was a family member, and horrifically enough, that "monster" ended up with only probation time!

As an adoptive parent, and past foster mom, I had personal dealings with similar cases, as I tried unsuccessfully to adopt most of the 72 children in my care over the span of 11 years. Unfortunately, some of the last several sibling-groups I was told would be adoptable, instead went right back to the offending parents, some right out of jail for domestic abuse charges. I was however, reassured that they had signed up for their "parenting classes", as if that would somehow comfort me?

My babies were being sent back to the same environment they were initially removed from, the babies I had bonded with, stayed up all night with, nursed through sickness, and treated as a family members, right along with my first adopted son, and the judge puts them right back into harms way? How does this happen in America? Needless to say, I voted in our last local election to remove every judge in our family courts, to be replaced by "gang prosecuting attorneys" running for their seat, and would recommend you do the same, if your local judges are as complacent as ours have been with our children! I refuse to believe that our precious children are reduced to nothing more than a dollar amount to those who keep circulating them through the Social Services System!

Another interesting news story about an America judge, who, while presiding over a case in June 2008, had to put himself under investigation due to the pornographic pictures of himself he had posted all over his website, which someone brought to his attention during an unrelated case he was presiding over. He was smart enough to know he had compromised his moral character, and therefore his ability to preside over the case, or even the capacity to be a judge.

And how moral is it to start a state lottery to help education and divert the funds to "other projects" and I'm positive it's not a project to put prayer back into our schools. Our Los Angeles public school teachers just recently staged an early morning strike, against job losses and pay cuts, fearing our "Governator" Arnold, had "shorted" them. However, at his follow-up press conference, the Governor stated, and I paraphrase, that he would be angry and striking too if he were a teacher, because the Los Angeles Unified School District Administration had paid out 150 million to consultants (not teachers), which had forced him to cut our budget.

I don't believe that the school teachers realized how much of their salaries and retirement had been squandered on so-called "consultants", and the Los Angeles Unified School District Administrators were really the ones to blame for the mismanagement of their funds. I have not heard of any reprimands over this betrayal to our teachers, who would be "fired" immediately if they brought their Christian faith to the public school classroom. Lower morals are working into every fiber of our nation, from the economy to the internet, and unfortunately our children are getting the worst of it!

CHAPTER 12

DISASTERS

America's declining morality is not our only problem however, and as discussed in prior chapters we are currently experiencing natural and made-made disasters at an absolutely unprecedented rate, unlike any other time in recorded history. Yes, I hear your scoffing, that in past times we haven't had the ability, nor the technology to record every single incident world-wide, to which I answer you're correct! All I can speak for is what I have actually witnessed and experienced in my 55 years, which started for me at the shaking of the ground at 3:05 a.m. on July 21, 1952, we witnessed one of only 7 (at that time) major earthquakes in Southern California. I was born <u>during</u> the Tehachapi Earthquake of 1952!

In my twenties I experienced the San Fernando/Simi Valley Earthquake. In my thirties, I moved to Hawaii, as the active volcano was erupting and devouring homes, landmarks, and highways. In my forties, the Northridge Quake thrust a new unknown vault into the air causing the mountains to tower several inches higher once the dust settled. My sister's house was on right on the epicenter. Those are only the big disasters (7.0 or higher on the Richter Scale), not even mentioning all the numerous tremors we have here, called before and after-shocks, and earthquake "swarms", up and down California state.

JUNE 2008

SAMARITAN'S PURSE® CRISIS RESPONSE UPDATE
from Franklin Graham

Responding to
Asia's Twin Catastrophes

DEAR FRIEND,

When the earthquake struck China on May 12, I was talking with several hundred seminary students in the port city of Nanjing, one of four Chinese cities I visited during a ten-day trip to this ancient land. I had no idea at the time of the magnitude of the quake to survive. Another woman was not so fortunate—she lost her only son.

As I was en route to China, Cyclone Nargis swept across Myanmar, killing as many as 135,000 people and leaving over 2 million homeless. Two days after the storm, Samaritan's Purse had

MORE >

MERCY FLIGHT. This 747 cargo jet, chartered by Samaritan's Purse, was the first privately chartered relief flight from the U.S. to arrive in Chengdu. It delivered 90 tons of desperately needed supplies.

California is also known for it's acres of forests, and tree-covered mountains, which every year catch fire, alternating North and South. Last year in 2007, most of San Diego County (our Southern most county, bordering Mexico to the South, and Orange County to the North), over a thousand homes, business, and open hills and fields were torched. This summer 2008, another huge area of redwood forest country is ablaze. I cannot even remember a year that there hasn't been a wildfire in California, some years are worse than others.

As bad as the natural disasters can be in California, the 911 attack on the Twin Towers in New York, 2001, and then Hurricane Katrina in 2005, left most of us devastated, unable to help or even get to our brothers and sisters as they were literally dying in front of our eyes on the news, made me realize we had entered a new phase in the earth's "birth-pangs" (Biblical reference to the end times). As soon as we could help we did, with relocations and any other way we could, yet curiously enough, it was the local services and national faith-based population and organizations who where the first responders on the scene.

Where was our government? The national guard stood by waiting for authorization that never came, and F.E.M.A. (Federal Emergency Management Agency, part of Homeland Security) officials, we heard tapes on the news, were trying to book dinner reservations at a popular restaurant, and wouldn't take anyone's calls. While our people were dying! Michael Brown, head of FEMA, was asked to step down shortly thereafter. Much to my horror, he went on about his business, becoming a consultant for disaster responses.

Disasters are striking globally on almost a monthly basis. In just the first six months of 2008, China had the worst winter snow in recorded history, earthquakes in Japan and China, volcanos erupting in Italy and Hawaii, back-to-back tornadoes followed by severe flooding in the mid-U.S. from the Great Lakes to the Gulf of Mexico, severe snow in the Northeast followed closely by severe heat (over 100 degrees), tornadoes and firestorms and drought in California, to name a few.

Add to all this, the "economic" storms of house foreclosures leaving millions of homes vacant, neighborhoods in ruin, families homeless, gas prices the highest in history, food-born illnesses (tomatoes or salsa ingredients) effecting hundreds of thousands throughout the U.S., food costs soaring, and they're afraid to say the "R" word? Recession hit last year, didn't anyone tell the economists or politicians? I believe 2008, has ushered in a depression.

And now for a real disaster, here are some depressing statistics; according to Bible Head Quarters online (I've rounded the statistics), since prayer was taken out of public schools in 1962, morality has nose-dived, divorce and adultery is up by 200 percent, sexually-transmitted diseases and suicide among teens is up 250 percent, unwed pre-teen mothers and unmarried couples living together is up 550 percent, violent crime is up 800 percent, and sexual abuse to children is up 2,000 percent! And again (I paraphrase) from Bible Head Quarters online, possibly the reason for everything (disasters) happening in America could be that, world-wide we're the number one pornography producer (including child porn), number one in teen suicides, pregnancies, drug use, divorce and violent crime.

PART IV

CONCLUSIONS

&

SOLUTIONS

"And evermore beside him on his way

the unseen Christ shall move;

Then he may lean upon his arm and say,

'Dost Thou, dear Lord approve?'"

- Henry Wadsworth Longfellow

American Center *for* Law & Justice

2008: YEAR OF DECISION

January 23, 2008, Washington, D.C. — From our strategically located headquarters in our nation's capital, directly across the street from the Supreme Court of the United States and moments from the Capitol, the ACLJ's legal and legislative teams work tirelessly to protect and preserve life and liberty, faithfully representing your values. This year's crucial issues and cases include:

Ten Commandments Under Fire

- Two Ten Commandments cases at the Supreme Court: *Summum v. Pleasant Grove City* and *Summum v. Duchesne City*
- Summum organization suing to force display of their "Seven Aphorisms"
- Option: Eliminate display of Ten Commandments
  - ACLJ reply briefs due within weeks

Christians Persecuted, Israel Threatened

- Countering claims of those pushing for peace by dividing the city of Jerusalem
- Move would appease terrorists and put Israel at serious risk
- Also opposing persecution against Christians by Hamas and other terrorist groups
- ACLJ Government Affairs and senior staff teaming with Chief Counsel Jay Alan Sekulow
- United Nations has agreed to our request for inquiry

Abortion Legalized?

- So-called "Freedom of Choice Act" would bar federal government regulation of abortion
- Would defy public polls, act of Congress and President, ruling of Supreme Court
- Passage would mean return of horrific partial-birth abortion practice now outlawed
- ACLJ working hard to see Freedom of Choice Act shelved

Pledge of Allegiance Targeted

- Freedom From Religion Foundation, represented by Dr. Michael Newdow, is suing Congress to remove "under God" from Pledge of Allegiance in *Freedom From Religion Foundation v. Congress*
- Single most serious anti-Pledge lawsuit in history
- Loss would likely lead to effective ban on God's name in public, including schools

Churches Intimidated Into Silence

- ACLJ actively engaged in fight to change "Johnson Amendment" law

(over)

CHAPTER 13

HELP IN TROUBLED TIMES

The statistics are troubling, violent crimes have been escalating, morality is declining, natural disasters are occurring at an accelerated pace and intensity, the stock market is at an all-time low and we are living in depressed times. If our prestigious universities were still teaching from the Biblical text, they would know that God's people flourish in times of famine (we're in a time of famine). Or if our children were still praying a morning prayer or had a moment of silence (hearing the prayers of others) in class would there really be a need to bring weapons to school? I think not!

When the faith-based organizations were getting through to the flood and hurricane victims in the Southern states with clean water, food, medicine, and clothing, I didn't see anyone refusing prayer or supplies. Likewise, in New York, strangers huddled together in prayer and tears, during and after the 911 attacks. In Indonesia and Sri Lanka, following their disasters, help from Christian aid-workers and volunteer doctors were not refused or shunned because of conflicting faiths. Prayers and hugs are almost always accepted by those who have no hope left, usually after total devastation.

frontlines

Inside

2 CBN Partners Unite in Prayer

6 Bringing Hidden Stories to Light

7 The Right Way to Start Your Day

Spread the Joy of Jesus in July

In Autumn, 2007, there had been such a severe drought in Georgia state that one of it's Mayors assembled his staff outside to pray for much-needed rain (to the dismay of the ACLU), and guess what, it rained! When we are at the end-of-our-rope, most of us will pray, and we always get the desired results (although sometimes not immediately)! A phrase I've heard repeated a lot lately which you may want to ponder and initiate, is:

"Little prayer --- little power,

Much prayer --- much power,

No prayer --- no power!"

A fitting song popular about 10 years ago, in which I can still visualize Jim Carey (helping out God, who's taken a vacation), strutting down the sidewalk in a scene from the Universal Picture "Bruce Almighty", 2003, the song blasted:

"I got the Power!

I got the Power!"

As hilariously funny as that movie was, imagine harnessing the power of God, without having to endure his enormous responsibilities in the process. Well, indeed we do have the ability to access God's love and wonderful healing power, no matter what area in your life needs healing, whether physical, financial, brokenness, loneliness, or protection, and it is absolutely free! Start with prayer, and end with prayer, because much prayer = much power!

I grew up feeling as though I didn't know how to pray, as I'm sure many others felt too, as you may remember we stopped praying at school when I was 10, so it must have been wrong, I thought. And those born later never had the privilege nor the protection of morning prayers, before the start of class each day. I thought I was unable to pray even though I grew up in the church, and was baptized. My grandmother taught Sunday School, so she did all the praying in my family, as my parents did not attend with us. I never really felt comfortable praying because I thought it wasn't cool enough, my parents didn't encourage it, and the schools completely cut-it-out. But God was still there, and is today, and he doesn't really care how we pray, but he wants to hear from you and me, every single day.

I was diagnosed with only 2 months to live at 38 years old, at which time I began to pray fervently, as did all my friends, and (coincidentally) it turned out to be a misdiagnosis. And I was thankful for everyone else's prayers too! They worked for me, as I've lived an additional 18, healthy and happy, years now. When your children are hurt or in trouble, you'll pray, and your prayers will be answered. It's free to try, so why not at least try - praying? It can't hurt, it can only help because God loves us and wants us to come to him with our every need, big or small. By answering our prayers, God gets to "show-off" (as our big, strong, Heavenly Father) and give us what we ask him for. How cool it that?

We need to be praying for our family, our friends, our pastors, our teachers, health-care workers, first-responders, elected officials, our President, and our nation (our Christian nation) if we're ever going to claim it back for the glory of God, and our children!

CHAPTER 14

RELIGIOUS FREEDOMS

How many of our God-given freedoms are you and I willing to give up permanently, before we ban together and do something? We have handed over our Christian heritage, our Judeo-Christian laws, our outward symbols of Christian adherence, our prayers and our children to the ACLU, the State, cultural tolerances, whether terroristic or perversive, and the new global or "world order".

Please correct me if I'm wrong, but does the new "world order" seem a bit like the old world order of Hitler's Nazi Germany? A global order at first appears to serve everyone equally (fairness doctrine), providing we are willing to submit, and give up our rights and religious freedoms, in lieu of the "good of all", yet it seems to me to be a sort of "take-over". I don't want to submit to non-Biblical rules and laws that I don't believe in, and I refuse to bow down to any other than Jesus, and I really do have a problem with this whole "global-order" take-over mentality, which has been infiltrating our society.

As a foster parent of 72 children over an 11-year span (in 2007, there were 20 children and babies in and out of my home), the majority of whom were court-ordered back to the

An Historical Perspective on the TEN COMMANDMENTS in AMERICAN LAW

THE FIFTH COMMANDMENT:
"Honor your father and mother..."

In the mid-seventeenth century, the colony of Connecticut passed a law that actually required children to obey their parents.

The Louisiana Court of Appeals reinforced this principle that children should obey their parents, when it wrote:

"Honor thy father and thy mother," is as much a command of the municipal law as it is a part of the Decalogue, regarded as holy by every Christian people. "A child," says the code, "whatever his age, owes honor and respect to his father and mother." [19]

Strong families are basic for social order in both secular and faith-based societies. Numerous studies from respected academics have documented that when the family breaks down, and along with it parental authority, the consequences for the future of society are largely negative.[20]

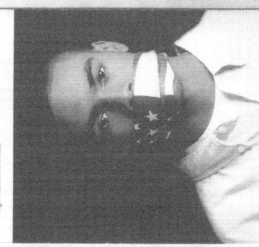

19 Sain v. Clancy, 187 So. 712, 728 (La. App. 1938) (citing Caldwell v. Hennen, 5 Rob. 20 (La. 1843)).
20 Two of the most respected academics in this field are David Popenoe and Barbara Defoe Whitehead of the Marriage Project at Rutgers University. For a detailed curriculum vitae of their work, go to http://marriage.rutgers.edu/codirector.htm.

"offending" parents or families they were originally removed from. I was warned against giving the children age-appropriate Bibles (in my Christian home), was repeatedly lied to and humiliated for wanting to help (share my home and heart), and admonished for verbalizing my desire to adopt more children. As if permanent, or habitual (repeat) foster care were good for children, families, or of any service to society, which it's NOT.

Did you see the news report about the break-away Mormon-sect living "Amishly" in Texas, intermarrying older men with multiple wives, including teen-aged girls? Four hundred children under the age of 18 were taken from their complex and painstakingly placed into foster care. More than half of the pre-teen and teen-aged girls were pregnant at the time of "removal", and the sect was investigated, although never charged with breaking laws of under-age marriages and sexually immoral activity between the men and teenaged girls. All the children were eventually returned to their home complex, standing on the First Amendment right of Religious Freedom to worship "their own way", and their spokesman said, they were even going to be more *"watchful and try"* to abide by the under-age *"laws"* of Texas from now on.

Wow, they knew they were breaking laws before, because now they were going to try harder to live by the law (laws the rest of us have to follow also). This, in our Judeo-Christian nation that cannot even pass laws protecting our children from internet porn and the resultant predators. Nor are our judges in fact, even capable of sentencing the perpetrators with an appropriate amount of jail-time prosecution (I believe three-years probation is the standard), because their only crime was damaging our "second-class-citizen" children? Please see what is happening to our country, please pray and start voting the "Christian" vote, as this is the only way we are going to get our nation back, back from the insanity going on all around us. The result of new-age "global-order", where everything is allowed in moderation, everything except Christianity's religious freedoms and freedom of expression.

CHAPTER 15

PRAYER BACK INTO PUBLIC SCHOOLS

In 1984, the Senate rejected a proposed constitutional amendment, supported by then current President Ronald Reagan, to permit organized, "spoken" prayers in the public schools. The Senate also voted down a proposed constitutional amendment to allow "silent" prayer in the public schools (Cummings, Milton, & Wise, 2001, p. 53).

Chuck Norris and his wife are the current spokespersons for teaching courses from the Bible (history and literature) in schools. This is not illegal, as the prejudicially un-informed may claim it to be. And the Equal Access Act of 1984 says basically, that if a federally funded high school allows clubs unrelated to the curriculum, they are required by law, to permit religious meetings, such as prayer and/or Bible clubs. In an online article at Liberty Magazine.org, entitled "Students, Teachers & Religious Freedom" by Haven Bradford Gow, 2005, he writes,

> *"According to Mathew Staver, a First amendment scholar and attorney and president of Liberty Counsel in Orlando, Florida, students and teachers need not sacrifice their First Amendment religious freedom rights once they enter a public school building. He observes that,"*

"according to the U.S. Constitution and U.S. Supreme Court decisions, students may engage in religious speech during noninstructional time; may distribute religious literature during noninstructional time (without having prior review and acceptance by school officials); may participate in free speech during class as long as the speech is compatible with the topic being studied; may give oral and written reports on religious topics as long as the report or presentation is consistent with the assignment or topic being studied; may establish Bible clubs as long as the school permits at least one other noncurriculum student organization.

Teachers likewise have First Amendment religious freedom rights. As Attorney Staver notes, teachers may exercise the right of free speech and religious freedom; may objectively and neutrally discuss religion as long as the discussion is consistent with the topic being taught; may use school facilities to meet with other school employees for religious purposes and receive equal treatment to that provided teachers for secular purposes; may bring in outside speakers to discuss religious topics or debate religious issues or moral issues from a religious perspective; may serve students as a Bible class sponsor.

Certainly religious students and teachers in the public schools need not be viewed and treated as second-class citizens."

According to the Center For Moral Clarity.net (CMC), they report that as of June 2007, the Department of Justice launched a program designed to protect religious rights in America, called the First Freedom Project (paraphrased). I'm not sure if it's "First" as in our nation's founding or referring to our "First" freedom the First Amendment, or both, and it doesn't matter what it stands for as long as they are doing something about protecting our religious freedoms. I sincerely hope they will be able to do something about reinstating prayer in our "federally funded" public schools in our Judeo-Christian nation! If not, I believe more Christians will pull their children out of public school to home school, if for no other reason, because of the safety and accountability issues, the quality-of-school (all public schools) is non-existent, until God and prayer go back to our schools.

A newsletter I received from my homeowner's insurance company in 2006, reported on home schooling statistics, that according to federal data from the National Center for Education Statistics, that the number of home schooled children rose almost 30 percent between 1999, and 2003, the very year my son started first grade. As discussed in an earlier chapter, within his first two weeks of public school I pulled him out because he'd been assaulted by an older student, and the school faculty failed to inform me. The news article continued about the main reasons other parents were home schooling their children citing their dissatisfaction with public education, due to concerns about the standardized (global) teaching, and a desire to maintain religious values and family unity.

Because It's Time To Take Back America

Here's what some great Christian leaders of the 20th Century said...

"Mat Staver is waging battle in America's courtrooms to stem the erosion of our inalienable rights recognized in the First Amendment. I am grateful he is on our side."
— D. James Kennedy, Ph.D., Founder, Coral Ridge Presbyterian Church

"I thank and praise our great God and Savior for Mat Staver and Liberty Counsel because they are standing in the gap to help defend our religious freedoms and civil liberties. I applaud their diligent efforts in the war against the precious rights given to us by God through our Founding Fathers and our Constitution."
— Bill Bright, Founder, Campus Crusade for Christ International

"I can think of no greater work being done right now in America for the sake of our religious freedom and Christian heritage than that being done by Liberty Counsel and its founder... Mathew Staver.
— Dr. Jerry Falwell, Founder, Liberty University

LIBERTY COUNSEL

WHAT TO PRAY FOR

THE CHURCH

Heavenly Father, we ask Y[ou] blessing on Your Church. [...] in us a renewed desire to [...] wholeheartedly, and to se[...] in Your Name. Grant us th[...] and wisdom to make an i[...] our nation and our world [...] glory. (Ephesians 4:3-6; 2 Thessalonians 1:4; Acts [...]

Specific requests:

- That the Church wou[ld] embrace and proclai[m] truth
- That God's people wo[uld] united
- That believers would [...] another and love the[...]
- That the Church wou[ld] characterized by inte[...] righteousness, throu[...] empowering of the H[...]

GOVERNMENT

Lord, we lift our elected le[aders] before You and ask that Y[ou] grant each one wisdom a[nd] discernment. We pray th[at] leaders would be bolster[ed]

Probably the most surprising resource I found on the topic of "putting prayer back into public schools" was the brief description of a book for sale on Amazon.com titled <u>Let Us Pray: A Plea for Prayer in Our Schools</u>, by William J. Murray, 1995. If you don't recognize his name, possibly you will remember his court case, cited in chapter 2 (he was the 14 year-old plaintiff, at that time):

<u>1963, Murray v. Curlett</u>

Supreme Court bans school prayer and Bible verse reading in the classrooms.

William Murray's book description from Circle.Adventist.org, reads,

> *"William J. Murray presents his argument for restoring voluntary prayer in schools, hoping to bring about freedom of religion not freedom from religion. Murray, an ordained minister in Texas and an outspoken advocate of prayer in U.S. public schools, now regrets his historic role as 14-year-old plaintiff in the case against the Baltimore school system that led to the Supreme Court's 1963 decision banning school prayer and Bible reading."*

I'll conclude with another quote, as I'm not the only concerned citizen regarding prayer in public schools or Christian religious rights for our children. A promotional phrase on a brochure for Pastor Rod Parsley's book <u>Culturally Incorrect</u>, 2007, states simply,

"We can RUN... We can HIDE... Or we can ENGAGE... CHOOSE."

REFERENCES

BOOKS

Allee, John Gage, Ph.D., 1986, <u>Webster's New Encyclopedia of Dictionaries</u>, "Dictionary of Presidents", Ottenheimer Publishers, Inc.

Barber, John, 2002, <u>America Restored</u>, Christian Focus Publications, FL

Catrow, David, 2002, <u>We the Kids</u>, Dial Books for Young Readers, NY

Cummings, Jr., Milton and Wise, David, 2001, <u>Democracy Under Pressure</u>, Nelson Thomson Learning, Canada

Cheney, Lynne, 2002, <u>America a Patriotic Primer</u>, Simon & Schuster Children's Publishing Division, NY

Disney, Walt, <u>Pinocchio</u>, 2000, Grolier Enterprises, CT

Ellis, Joseph J., 2007, <u>American Creation</u>, Random House, NY

Fink, Sam, 2002, <u>The Declaration of Independence</u>, Scholastic Inc., NY

Gingrich, Newt, 2006, <u>Rediscovering God in America</u>, Integrity Publishers, TN

Hagee, John, 2006, <u>Jerusalem Countdown</u>, FrontLine, FL

Hanna, Sharon L., 2000, <u>Person to Person</u>, Prentice Hall, NJ

Isaacson, Walter, 2007, <u>Einstein</u>, Simon & Schuster, New York, NY

Kennedy Dean, Jennifer, 2005, <u>Fueled by Faith</u>, New Hope Publishers, AL

Kjos, Berit, 1995, <u>Brave New Schools</u>, Harvest House Publishers, OR

Lucado, Max, General Editor, 1995, <u>The Inspirational Study Bible</u>, NKJV, Word Publishing, U.S.A.

Mangione, Peter L., Editor, 1995, <u>A Guide to Culturally Sensitive Care, Infant/Toddler Caregiving</u>, California Dept. of Education

McCullough, David, 2001, <u>John Adams</u>, Simon & Schuster, NY

Morgan, Robert J., 2003, <u>Then Sings My Soul</u>, Thomas Nelson, Inc., TN

New King James Version, 1995, <u>The Inspirational Study Bible</u>, Word Publishing

Parsley, Rod, 2007, <u>Culturally Incorrect</u>, Thomas Nelson, Inc., TN

Robertson, Pat, 2004, <u>Courting Disaster</u>, Integrity Publishers, a division of Integrity Media, Inc., TN

Rubel, David, 2005, <u>Encyclopedia of The Presidents and Their Times</u>, Scholastic Inc., NY

Stone, Perry, 2005, <u>Unusual Prophecies Being Fulfilled</u>, Voice of Evangelism, Inc., TN

MAGAZINES & EDUCATIONAL POSTERS

Inland Empire Family Magazine, January, 2005, "Spiritual Education, How Religion is a Tool to Teaching the Whole Child", Laurie, Greg, "Bibles on Campus, The Conflict: School Means Freedom, and of Religion", Leuer, Jennifer

The Mini Page Poster, 1991, "The Bill of Rights", Debnam, Betty

MOVIES
- "Bruce Almighty", 2003, Universal Pictures
- "Expelled, No Intelligence Allowed", 2008, Ben Stein & Premise Media Corp.
- "Fantasia", 1950's, Walt Disney Production
- "Ferris Bueller's Day Off", 1986, Paramount Pictures Corporation
- "First Landing", 2006, CBN/Regent University Production

TELEVISION
- Breakthrough, (Theme: Conference featuring John Ashcroft), December, 2005
  - (Theme: Margaret Sanger's Planned Parenthood), May, 2008
- CBN 700 Club, (Theme: California Textbooks Sensitivity Guidelines), 1/2005
  - (Theme: 400 Yr. Anniv. Missionaries Landing VA Beach), 4/2005
  - (Theme: Textbook Agendas), Summer, 2005
  - (Theme: Jews Against Anti-Christian Defamation), 12/2005
  - (Theme: War on Christmas book), 12/2005
  - (Theme: Judicial Activism on Separation Church/State), 1/2006
  - (Theme: The New Atheism with David Aikman), 5/2008
- "CSI", (Theme: School Bullies), rerun of 1991 TV series, airing 1/2005
- Creation in the 21st Century, (Theme: Evolution and Race), Fall, 2005
- Fox Nightly News, (Theme: Pennsylvania Intelligent Design Case), January, 2005
- Religion & Ethics Newsweekly, (Theme: Confusion over Holiday/Christmas) PBS, December, 2005
- TBN Special, (Theme: The Signature of God, program hosted by Grant Jefferies, based upon his book of the same name), Fall, 2005
  - (Theme: Separation of Church & State, with Congressman, Dan Roerbacker), January, 2006
  - (Theme: A Spiritual Heritage Tour of the U.S. Capitol, hosted by David Barton of Wall Builders), repeated May, 2008
  - (Theme: Founding Fathers Special), July 4, 2008

WEBSITES (www)
- ABC News.com/dailynews.att.net/Headline-"Judge Rules Against Pa. Biology Curriculum", 2005
- ACLJ.org (American Center For Law and Justice.org)/In the News-
  - Associated Press - "Lawsuit Seeks Removal of Crosses from Las Cruses, NM City Logo", AP, 2005
  - Washington Times - "Religion Under a Secular Assault", Duin, Julia, 2005
- ACHW.org/American Christian Heritage Week Ministries
  - "The Separation of Church and State"
- Agape Press.org/From the Home Front, Headlines
  - "2006: A Year of Love", Jimenez, Jane, 2006
- American Athiest.org/courthouse/ "A Decline in American Culture Due to Lack of Religion?", Lee, David, 2005
- BibleHeadQuarters.org "Proof Jesus is Coming Very Soon", Bartlett, Adam, 1998

WEBSITES, (www. continued)
- CBN News.com/Spiritual Life - Religion Roundup, Christian World News, 2005
  - "Ache: Christians Still Help; Muslims Grateful to Christians",
  - "Battleground: Public Schools and the Gay Agenda"
  - "Churches, Christian Groups Reach Out to Help Katrina Victims"
  - "Churches Playing Key Role in Massive Relief Effort"
  - "Christians Comfort Tsunami Victims"
  - "Christians Sending Relief to Quake Victims"
  - "Criminalization of Christianity", Griffith, Wendy, 2005
  - "Evolution: Science or Atheism in Disguise?"
  - "Faith-Based Groups United in Relief Response", CWNews, 2005
  - "Mercy Ships: Giving Relief to Katrina and Rita Victims"
    - Martin, Steve, 2005
  - "OB Supplies Medicine to Evacuees in Baton Rouge"
    - Stakelbeck, Erick, 2005
  - "Pilgrims Planted the First Seeds of Faith in America"
  - "Saudi Arabia: Christians Imprisoned/Beaten for Worshiping Jesus"
  - "Sri Lanka's Christians Help Tsunami Survivors"
    - Thomas, George, 2005
  - "Supreme Question: Considering the Ten Commandments"
    - Strand, Paul, 2005
  - "Tempers Flare Over Intelligent Design Curriculum"
    - Sitton, Darla, 2005
  - "Tsunami Relief Reaching Remote Areas", Esteban, Jay, 2005
  - "What's The Big Secret?", Earley, Mark, 2005
  - "Will the U.S. Protect Religious Freedoms Worldwide?"
    - Lane, Gary, 2005
- California State Library @ library.ca.gov/"History and Culture", founded 1850
- Center For Moral Clarity.net/Media Center,
  - "Founding Fathers Speak Out About God" Backgrounder, 2006
  - "Statement on Pledge Ruling", Parsley, Rod, 2005
- Circle.Adentist.org/browse/resource.phtml?leaf <u>Let us Pray: A Plea for Prayer in Our Schools</u>, Murray, William J., 1995
- Creation Evidence.org/books, <u>Why do Men Believe Evolution -Against All Odds?</u>, Ch.10, "Why Good Men Believe Bad Science", Baugh, Carl E., 1999
- Encarta.msn.com/"1960: Crime and Crime Prevention: Crime Statistics", 2005
- Faith and Action.org/"A Historic Example of Judicial Activism: The Cantwell Case", New, David W., Esq., 2005
- First Amendment Center.org/analysis "Plaintiff in 1962 Landmark School-Prayer Case Reflects on His Role", Hudson, David Jr., 2005
- Freedom Forum.org/"Education for Freedom Lesson 9 - Tests Used by the Supreme Court in Establishment Clause"

WEBSITES, (www, continued)
    Liberty Magazine.org/ "By What Authority?", McClintock, Tom, United States Senator, 2002
        "Evolution and Intelligent Design", &
        "Students, Teachers, & Religious Freedom",
            Gow, Haven Bradford, 2005
        "Indispensable Supports", From the Farewell Address of President George Washington, 1796
        "Teach Us to Pray", Standish, Timothy G., Ph.D., 2005
    Missions of California.org/foundation
        "The California Missions", 2000
        "Response to the Lawsuit Filed by Americans United for Separation of Church and State to Block the California Missions Preservation Act", 2004
    PBS.org/ "A Space Odyssey: People & Discoveries", "Albert Einstein", 2005
    PIP For Schools.com/Student's Corner - Hero's of Faith
        "Do You Know About Dr. Benjamin Rush?", 2004
    Stateline.org/"Your Governor Wishes You a (fill in the blank)"
        Kelderman, Eric, 2005
    SamaritansPurse.org/MP_Articles, 2005
        "Franklin Graham Tours Devastated Area"
        "Ministering to Earthquake Survivors"
        "Overcoming the Tsunami"
        "Storm Leaves Thousands Homeless in Central America"
    Trinity Broadcasting Network - TBN.org, "Aid to New Orleans", 2005
    Under God ProCon.org/Historical Background, 2005
        "References to God in State Constitutions"
        "First Amendment of the U.S. Constitution" & "U.S. Flag Code"
        "Founding Fathers" & "Religion in the Colonies"
        "How Did Religion Influence the American Colonies"
        "Pledge History" & "Was the U.S. Founded 'Under God'?"
        "References to God in State Constitutions"
    Wall Builders.com/Resources/ Barton, David
        "A Tale of Two Constitutions", 2004
        "God: Missing in Action from American History", 2005
        "Letters Between the Danbury Baptists and Thomas Jefferson", 1801 - 1802
        "Revisionism: How to Identify It In Your Children's Textbooks", 2003
        "Solving the Pledge of Allegiance Controversy", 2003
        "Thomas Paine Criticizes the Current Public School Science Curriculum", 2003
    Wikipedia.org/ "Christian Right", 2005

ILLUSTRATIONS & DOCUMENTS/REPRINTS

ACLJ (American Center for Law & Justice), "2008: Year of Decision" brochures, 2008
ACLU (American Civil Liberties Union.org), "Religious Liberty-Press Releases"
    for years 1999-2005
American Defense Fund, "10 Commandments in American Law" brochure, 2005
"America the Beautiful", Song, 1893
    Katherine Lee Bates/Lyrics, Samuel A. Ward/Music
    Morgan, Robert, 2003, Then Sings My Soul
    Thomas Nelson, Inc., TN
"A World in Need", website of Christian Contractors Association.org
Barrows, Marjorie, A Book of Famous Poems, 1931, "Beatitudes & Psalm 91", copied
    from pages 114/115, Whitman Publishing, WI
Bryan, William Jennings, The World's Famous Orations, Vol. V, 1906, Funk & Wagnalls
    Co., NY, copy of page 119, "Spurgeon"
City of Claremont, "Calendar of Special Events", 2005, Claremont Human Services
Cook, R.J., One Hundred and One Famous Poems, 1924, The Cable Company, IL,
    Copies of pages 175/176, & 183, "The Ten Commandments",
    "Magna Charta", and "Choosing Books for Children"
Darwin, Charles, (1809-1882) reprinted from www.Infidels.org/Library/Historical
    On the Origin of Species, "Introduction", 1859, &
    Decent of Man, Ch.VII - "On the Races of Man", 1871
Disney, Walt, Pinocchio, 2000, reprints of pages 1, 23 & 24, Grolier Enterprises, CT
"First Landing", CBN movie poster, 2007
"Freedoms Calendar, 2007-2008", reprints of "July/Statue of Liberty" &
    "December/Bible & U.S. Flag", American Bible Society
"Frontlines", CBN monthly magazine covers, May & July, 2007
Gibson, John, The War on Christmas, 2005, promotional picture and write-up from
    Crossings Book Club, 2006
"Holidays Around the World" pictures and text, Griggs Lawrence, Robin
    "Easy Magazine", holiday 2005
Kelly, Reverend M.V., C.S.B., A Catechism of Christian Doctrine, 1929, John P. Daleden
    Co., IL, copy of "Title Pages" & "Preface"
"Liberty Ideals Magazine", 1946
    "Around the Flag Pole", Cover Picture, Hinke, Geo.
    "First Stars & Stripes on the Ocean -1777", Painting, DeLand, Clyde
    "For Their Sake", Painting, American Red Cross
    "Lincoln Memorial w/Text" & "Minute-Man Statue", Hooper, Van B.
    "Statue of Liberty w/Text", Hooper, Van B.
    "Statue of Liberty", Drawing, Hollrock
National Archives Publication, Charters of Freedom, 1952, reprint of original, 1776,
    "The unanimous Declaration of the thirteen united States of America"
"Petition to Protect Military Prayer", American Center for Law & Justice (ACLJ.org)
    Copy of signed petition, 2005

ILLUSTRATIONS & DOCUMENTS/REPRINTS (continued)

"Petition to the U.S. Supreme Court to Return to the Intended Meaning of the First Amendment", Coral Ridge Ministries, FL, 2005
    Copy of my signed petition, 2005
Phillips, Reverend M., The Baltimore Catechism, 1911, Frank H. Kirner, Publisher, PA,
    Copy of original "Cover" & "Index"
"Reclaiming the Covenant", CBN Certificate, my copy, 2007
Rush, Dr. Benjamin, (1745-1813) reprint from BibleBelivers.com/Bible_in_Schools
    "A Defence of the Use of the Bible in Schools", 1830
    American Tract Society, TX
    The New England Primer, 1777, reprinted from
    My.Voyager.net/~jayjo/primer
Schwarzenegger, Arnold, 2005, (hand painted Christmas card), printed from Stateline.org article "Your Governor Wishes You a (fill in the blank)",
    Kelderman, Eric, 2005
Seal of Los Angeles County, "before and after" changes, 2008
"The Value of the College at Princeton", 1754, by Samuel Davis & Gilbert Tennent
    Reprinted from American Colonist's Library @ Princeton.html
"Through the Country Door", Autumn, 2005, mail-order catalog photo of "U.S. Flag" patchwork quilt for order
Washington, George, "Thanksgiving Proclamation", 1789, reprinted from CBN.com
    "Indispensable Supports", 1796, From the Farewell Address
    reprinted from LibertyMagazine.org/

Made in the USA
Lexington, KY
01 February 2013